In Canadian Service
Aircraft

Canadair CF-5
FREEDOM FIGHTER

Photo Opposite: CF-5D 116814 starting up on the ramp at CFB Trenton.

(Richard J. de Launais)

In Canadian Service
Aircraft

Canadair CF-5
FREEDOM FIGHTER

Anthony L. Stachiw
with Andrew Tattersall

Vanwell Publishing Limited
St. Catharines, Ontario

Vanwell Publishing acknowledges the financial support of the Government of Canada through the Book Publishing Industry Development Program for our publishing activities.

Vanwell Publishing acknowledges the Government of Ontario through the Ontario Media Development Corporation's Book Initiative.

Cover Design: Simon Baker
Cover Painting: Detail from "Last Run of the Moose" by Randall Whitcomb
Book Design: Renée Giguère

Vanwell Publishing Limited
1 Northrup Crescent
P.O. Box 2131
St. Catharines, Ontario L2R 7S2
sales@vanwell.com
tel: 905-937-3100
fax: 905-937-1760
Printed in Canada

National Library of Canada Cataloguing in Publication

Stachiw, A. L. (Anthony L.), 1940-
    Canadair CF-5 Freedom Fighter / Anthony L. Stachiw with Andrew Tattersall.

(In Canadian service. Aircraft)
Includes bibliographical references.
ISBN 1-55125-073-X

    1. F-5 (Jet fighter plane). 2. Fighter planes–Canada. 3. Canada.
Canadian Armed Forces–Aviation. I. Tattersall, Andrew, 1971- II. Title.
III. Series.

UG1242.F5S73 2003   358.4'383'0971   C2003-902162-9

CONTENTS

ACKNOWLEDGEMENTS

There are several people whose assistance has been instrumental in writing this book. I would like to thank John Griffin, the noted authority on Canadian military aircraft, and author of several books on the subject, for his encouragement and support. John Turanchik, whose keen eye for detail has, over the years, provided clippings from newspapers and magazines whenever he spotted material relevant to the CF-5 aircraft. MWO Luc Peladeau of the Directorate of Disposals, Sales, and Loans, Department of National Defence (DND), provided direction to the DDSAL website for confirmation of data on the CF-5 fleet disposal as well as the aircraft configuration as they were offered for sale.

The staff of The Canadian Forces Joint Imagery Centre, A Squadron, DND, in particular Janet Lacroix and WO Steve Sauvé, provided assistance and direction in the procurement of the photographs. The approval for their use was expedited by Simmy Chauhan and Armanda Tomei of the Directorate of Intellectual Property, DND.

Both Richard De Launais and Patrick Martin have provided several photographs from their extensive collections. Photographs by Robert Bryden, Peter Foster, John Lumley, Greg Marshall, and Steve Sauvé, are also featured. Patrick Martin's publication, Canadian Armed Forces, Aircraft Finish & Markings, 1968-1997, was used as an indispensable guide in writing Chapter 5, "CF-5 Colour Schemes and Markings."

Several people provided material for Chapter 7 on "Modelling the CF-5 Freedom Fighter." John Lumley, Vic Schuerman, and Bill Scobie provided photographs of the excellent models they had constructed of the CF-5, and James Botiatis of JBOT Decals, Mike Grant of Mike Grant Decals and Dave Koss of Leading Edge Models provided information on their decal products depicting the markings for the CF-5 Freedom Fighter.

Finally, thanks to Simon Kooter of Vanwell Publishing for providing the opportunity to present this book, and to Angela Dobler, the editor, for her expertise in its preparation.

CHAPTER ONE

Origins of the Design Northrop N156F

The first Northrop N-156F 59-4987 (YF-5A) prototype in flight over the Mojave Desert in California.

(Museum of Flight, Seattle, Washington)

In the early 1950s the Northrop Corporation initiated a program for the development of a supersonic lightweight fighter design. The company was, at the time, producing the F-89 Scorpion interceptor, certainly the largest and most costly fighter ever to serve with the USAF up to that time. It was recognized that initial procurement cost was not the only factor to be considered: research and development, and maintenance and operation of the system were factors that were putting the fighters then being developed or produced out of reach of Allied nations as potential customers.

In an attempt to stop the ever increasing size, weight, complexity and cost that appeared necessary to achieve the advances in performance as experienced in the emerging "Century Series" fighters, the design team, headed by Welko E. Gasich, was directed to produce a much less costly design. The initial concept, designated N-109 Fang, was inaugurated in December 1952, and appeared as a mockup in September 1953. This proposed single seat high altitude fighter emerged with a thin shoulder mounted delta wing, a low-set horizontal tail, and a swept back vertical tail. The turbojet powerplant, intended to be either the Armstrong

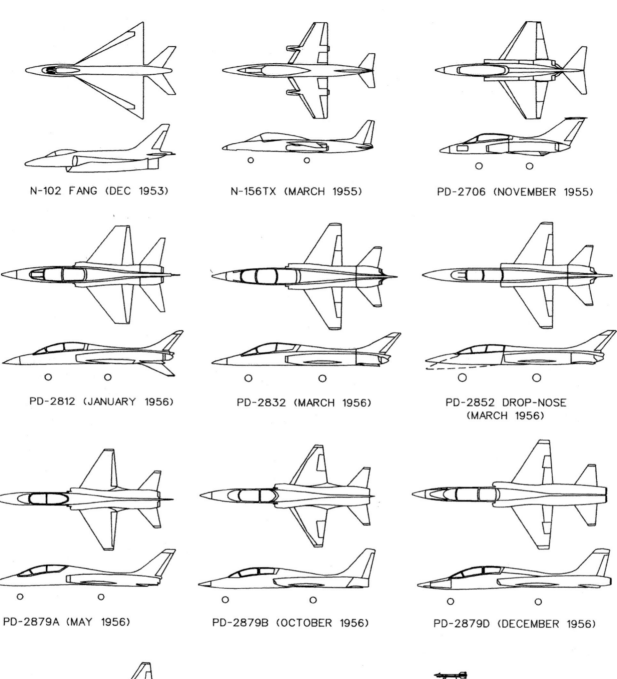

N-102 FANG (DEC 1953)

N-156TX (MARCH 1955)

PD-2706 (NOVEMBER 1955)

PD-2812 (JANUARY 1956)

PD-2832 (MARCH 1956)

PD-2852 DROP-NOSE
(MARCH 1956)

PD-2879A (MAY 1956)

PD-2879B (OCTOBER 1956)

PD-2879D (DECEMBER 1956)

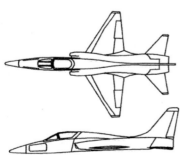

N-156F (OCTOBER 1956)

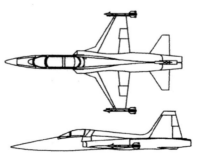

YF-5A ROLL-OUT (MAY 30 1959)

Siddeley J65 or the General Electric J79, was mounted in the lower aft fuselage fed by a ventral intake below the pilot's cockpit, not unlike the current F-16 Falcon fighter. The fighter, with a wing loading of 55 lb/sq.ft., weighing 15,000 - 18,000 lb., was considered lightweight by comparison to then current designs. It would have had a top speed of Mach 2 with the J79 engine, and a zoom ceiling nearing 70,000 ft. The impetus for the design philosophy was in reaction to discussions with the USAF regarding their experience in the Korean War. As it turned out, the Lockheed Aircraft Corporation had similar discussions which were to result in the design of the F-104 Starfighter. As a consequence, the Northrop project advanced no further, although it nevertheless influenced Northrop design efforts.

The design concept which resulted in the N-156 family was the result of studies conducted in early 1954. Discussion with officials in the North Atlantic Treaty Organization (NATO) and South East Asia Treaty Organization (SEATO) countries revealed concern with the escalating costs of weapon systems, compromising effectiveness of defence capabilities within existing budgets. The difficulty of maintaining this increasingly complex equipment in the field was another major concern.

The design team considered employing a family of small, high thrust-to-weight ratio turbojet engines under development at General Electric. The J-85 family, originally intended as short life engines for missile application, had a promising potential for powering small supersonic fighter designs. A preliminary design was quickly formulated to be powered by a pair of the new engines. Named the Tally-Ho, the baby fighter project received added impetus when, in May 1955, the USAF Air Training Command issued a general operational requirement for a supersonic trainer aircraft to replace the Lockheed T-33 subsonic trainer aircraft. The original concept, featuring the engines mounted in pods under an unswept wing, was greatly refined in 1955 by moving the engines into the fuselage and increasing the length, resulting in a much heavier and faster aircraft with a projected Mach 1.5 performance.

At this time, the U.S. Navy issued a requirement for a fighter to fly Combat Air Patrols from the light carriers that could not accommodate the McDonnell F3H Demon or Vought F8U Crusader then in service. To meet this requirement, the wing was lowered on the fuselage, a short coupled T-tail was adopted, and large flaps were fitted. Wing loading was minimized in keeping with the carrier requirement, and a relatively compact size was maintained in consideration of the small storage area of the jeep carriers.

The decision of the U.S. Navy in March 1956 to mothball the light carrier fleet nullified the requirement for a light fighter. However, the potential for a similar design for NATO and SEATO application, which had been researched by Northrop, prompted them to persist in this direction. The N-156, as the design became known, was modified with the latest state of the art concepts. Area rule was applied to the fuselage, which was also lengthened to improve the fineness ratio. Cambered leading edges were applied to the wing, which was mounted low on the fuselage, and a large retractable ventral fin for use in supersonic flight was added, along with a booster rocket.

The USAF's supersonic trainer design requirement had resulted in the N-156 design being split into the N-156T trainer oriented requirement, and the N-156F fighter. In June 1956 the Northrop design was announced as the winner of the trainer competition, and since no interest had been apparent in the fighter, the trainer design and development took priority. The wing area was reduced and the platform revised. The ventral fin was eliminated in favour of a larger vertical tailplane with reduced sweep back. A mechanically drooping nose section to reduce frontal area while providing adequate forward vision for the rear seat instructor was considered, then rejected, because of the added weight and complexity. Instead, the fuselage was given an elongated S-shaped profile with a cambered forward fuselage and concave underside. The roots of the wing trailing edge were filleted, the wing taper increased, and other small detail refinements made and incorporated in a full scale mockup.

The first YT-38, serial no. 58-1191, powered by non-afterburning YJ85GE-1 engines, flew for the first time on 10 April 1959. In all, six YT-38s were built, the final three powered by YJ85-GE-5 engines with afterburning. Testing was very promising, and approval for production was given in December, 1956 for four, then an additional thirteen aircraft under the designation T-38, and the name Talon was adopted for the aircraft. Deliveries began in March 1961, and when production ceased in 1972, 1187 aircraft had been built.

Although the trainer had, by necessity, been given the better part of the design office attention, by no means had the N-156F fighter been entirely ignored. Continuing as a company funded project, the fighter progressed with every effort being made to retain a basic structure common to the trainer. Necessary design changes were confined to the forward fuselage. Both variants were exhaustingly tested in a wind tunnel to prove the design before any actual flight testing was undertaken.

Because of the basic differences in performance requirements, certain changes were incorporated in the fighter variant. New engine air intakes were developed for the higher speeds envisioned for the fighter, as well as extended wing leading edge roots to improve wing performance. Leading edge flaps were provided to increase the maximum lift coefficient to accommodate higher gross weights.

In May 1958 these efforts met with some success when the USAF, acting on behalf of the US Department of Defense, issued a $32 million development contract for three flight test aircraft, serialled 59-4987 to 59-4989, and one static test prototype aircraft, serial 59-4993 (the prototype YF-5A serial no. 59-4987 is held today as part of the Museum of Flight, Air and Space Collection in Seattle, Washington).

Because of the basic commonality with the T-38 Talon, the first fighter was rolled out just over a year later on 30 May 1959. The first flight was on 30 July under the hand of Northrop test pilot Lew Nelson from Edwards Air Force Base in California. Although this aircraft was powered by non-afterburning YJ85-GE-1 engines, the thoroughbred characteristics of the diminutive aircraft were demonstrated when it achieved supersonic speed. Cannon armament was installed later and after 32 flights, the original engines were replaced by production J85-GE-5 versions each rated at

2,500 lb. static thrust dry, and 3,850 lb. static thrust with afterburning. The second aircraft joined the flight test program in January 1960, but, the completion of the third aircraft, which was to have joined the program in March 1960, was deemed unnecessary and it was placed in storage. This aircraft was to have had full weapon system capability.

In-the-field maintenance tests were conducted, and rough-field operations and operations from an unprepared strip took place at NAS Pensacola. Test firings of Sidewinder, Sparrow III, and Falcon air-to-air missiles were made, and drops of various externally mounted ordnance such as bombs, unguided rockets, napalm tanks and Bullpup air-to-surface missiles took place. As well, a test with a 2000-lb "special weapons shape" (tactical nuclear weapon) on the centerline was conducted. The aircraft could carry a heavier load than the F-100 Super Sabre and had a higher speed, better airfield performance, and a lower fuel consumption rate. Nevertheless, at the conclusion of the flight test program in August of 1960, the USAF decided that there was no immediate requirement for the aircraft, and the entire program was shelved.

Nevertheless, in May 1962 the N-156F was selected by the Department of Defense to be provided to favoured nations under the Military Assistance Program. Northrop were to produce two versions of the N-156F, designated F-5A

USAF T-38 Talon aircraft, the first supersonic trainer aircraft, still in active service.
(A. Stachiw)

The first prototype N-156F 59-4987 at the Museum of Flight at Seattle Washington prior to refurbishment and display, 21 July 1984.

(Patrick Martin)

in single seat form, and F-5B as a two seat variant. The F-5B was a dual operational aircraft and differed from the T-38 Talon in many respects, while retaining that aircraft's basic configuration. The first official order for 71 F-5A and 15 F-5B aircraft was placed in October 1962. While the N-156F had been conceived as an air superiority fighter, as the F-5, its operational mission potential was broadened, and it came to be supplied as a counter air fighter with many detail modifications and changes of equipment.

Originally, the USAF had displayed no interest in the lightweight fighter, and the F-5 was intended for the MAP only. However the USAF requested some 200 aircraft for service in Vietnam as a result of the high attrition rate in aircraft employed there, due to the availability of the new fighter. The request was turned down by the Defense Department, but approval was given in July 1965 for an evaluation program code named "Skoshi Tiger". The USAF was loaned twelve combat ready F-5A fighters from MAP inventory, consisting of five F-5A-15 and seven F-5A-20 variants, which were assigned to the 4503rd Tactical Fighter Wing. The 4503rd Tactical Fighter

Squadron (Provisional) was formed on 29 July 1965 for operational evaluation, the pilots being trained at Williams AFB. The unit was renamed 10th Fighter Commando Squadron, attached to the 3rd Tactical Fighter Wing at Bien Hoa Airbase in Vietnam.

Northrop modified the aircraft for service in South East Asia with ninety pounds of armour installed on the belly of the aircraft, inflight refuelling probe on the port side of the nose, and jettisonable pylons under the wings. Instruments were modified, and a lead computing gunsight installed. The travel limiter was removed from the rudder and flight controls were modified. In this configuration, the aircraft was designated F-5C.

These aircraft arrived at Bien Hoa Airbase, South Vietnam on 23 October 1965, having departed Williams AFB on 20 October. Combat missions were flown the same day. The unit strength was later increased to eighteen aircraft with the arrival of six more F-5As. The fighter was employed in close support, interception, and reconnaissance missions, typically carrying loads of 2000 - 3000 lbs. of ordnance.

The bomb aiming and delivery system of the F-5A was relatively unsophisticated, and its load carrying ability was not comparable to the F-4 Phantom II or the F-105 Thunderchief. However, it was fast and manoeuverable while making its bombing run in a shallow dive, the pilot using his lead computing gunsight to estimate the range. The aircraft proved to be the least vulnerable to ground fire in that conflict, only two of the aircraft having been lost on operations. The aircraft were never operated over North Vietnam, so the air to air capability was never tested.

The aircraft was not without shortcomings. With a heavy ordinance load, the takeoff roll was excessively long, but this was later remedied by the provision of a two-position nosewheel leg. Difficulty was experienced with the dropping of certain ordinance, in particular the 750 napalm tank, which on occasion failed to separate cleanly and struck the underside of the wing. Other problems were experienced with the 20mm cannon armament. These and other problems were eventually solved by cooperation between the USAF ground crew and Northrop representatives, and the F-5 achieved the lowest maintenance time per flight hour of any aircraft in Vietnam operations.

In spite of its technical and operational success, the career of the F-5 with the USAF was relatively short. The decision was made against further acquisition of the fighters, and the surviving F-5As were turned over to the South Vietnamese Air Force, which eventually operated some 126 of the type in four squadrons, and later three squadrons equipped with F-5E Tiger II aircraft. Northrop-built F-5 aircraft eventually were to enter service with Ethiopia, Greece, Iran, Jordan, Korea, Libya, Morocco, Norway, Philippines, South Vietnam, Taiwan, Thailand, Turkey, and the Yemen Arab Republic. As well, the F-5 was produced in Spain under licence by Construcciones Aeronauticas S.A. (CASA) for the Ejercito del Aire. Engines were built by General Electric in the United States.

Licenced production in Canada by Canadair Ltd. at Cartierville in the Montreal area was undertaken for the Canadian Armed Forces and the Royal Netherlands Air Force. The engines, designated J-85-CAN15, were produced by Orenda Ltd. at Malton, Ontario. When, as a result of a change in defence policy a number of CF-5 aircraft were declared surplus to operational requirement, they were placed in storage at the Air Maintenance Development Unit facility at Canadian Forces Base Trenton. These were to be rotated in service to maintain an equal number of hours on the airframes. Of these aircraft, eighteen were subsequently

sold to Venezuela. In order to meet the training requirements of the Canadian Forces twenty new-build CF-5Ds were produced of which two went to Venezuela as well.

In 1968 the USAF began to consider a successor to the F-5 under a continuation of the Military Assistance Program. An Improved International Fighter Aircraft for supply to allied and friendly nations from 1971 onwards was proposed. Some eight companies were invited to submit proposals based on existing designs. The field was narrowed to versions of the F-104 Starfighter, F-8 Crusader, A-4 Skyhawk, F-4 Phantom, and the F-5 Freedom Fighter. Eventually, the developed version of the F-5, the F-5E Tiger II was selected.

The F-5E and the two-seat F-5F evolved from an engineering design change proposed by Northrop, and included all the improvements incorporated in the F-5 over its production life. These included the two-position nose gear, demisted windscreen, and short field equipment. As well, additional fuel capacity was provided in the fuselage, new air intake ducts to accommodate the greater air volume requirements of the more powerful engines, and a wider and reprofiled fuselage. A wing with greater span and area was developed featuring new leading edge root extensions, manoeuvering flaps linked to the throttle lever buttons, and provision of hard points to accommodate increased underwing weapons stores. Miniature X-Band nose radar and a central air data computer were also installed. The first F-5E was flown on 11 August 1972.

The first production aircraft were delivered to the 425th Tactical Fighter Squadron of the USAF based at Chandler AFB in Arizona to provide conversion training for pilots of recipient nations. Following production was to supply designated friendly nations. The USAF and U.S. Navy also equipped special units to act as aggressors in training their pilots to combat potential enemies. This selection was made on the basis of the similarity of the F-5E/F to variants of the MiG-21 in both size and performance.

The F-5E/F remained in production until 16 January 1987, when the last two were delivered, although a few more were assembled from spares, the last of these being delivered on 29 June 1989. Northrop built a total of 792 F-5E, 140 F-5F, and 12 RF-5E. FFA in Switzerland assembled 90 F-5E and F-5F, Korean Air built 68, and AIDC of Taiwan built 380 aircraft. The F-5E/F series was not adopted by Canada, which eventually chose the CF-18 Hornet as its replacement for the CF104 Starfighter and CF101 Voodoo aircraft.

CHAPTER TWO

The CF-5 in Canadian Service

The first CF-5A, serial no. 116701, undergoing flight testing at Edwards AFB in California.
(Canadair Ltd.)

The 1964 Canadian Government White Paper on Defence assigned top priority to the development of a force of highly mobile and flexible land and air units, capable of deploying rapidly to any troubled area of the world for active peacekeeping under the aegis of the United Nations, or for any other employment in support of our NATO or other commitments. Mobile Command, as it was named, became the centrepiece of the Canadian military organization. Coincident with the minister's announcement, the integration of the armed forces was initiated. When this initiative was completed, a balanced force necessary to meet the increasing demands being made on Canada for peacekeeping and peace-restoring duties would be in place.

In 1965 the RCAF issued a requirement for a new tactical support fighter aircraft to be used to equip squadrons assigned to Mobile Command then being formed. For economic reasons, it was accepted that the development of a Canadian attack fighter was unsound, and that the selection of an existing foreign design modified to the requirements of this tasking was the answer. Submissions were received for some fourteen types of aircraft. The RCAF expressed preference for the Republic F-105 Thunderchief, the massive

USAF fighter bomber which was distinguishing itself in the Vietnam operations. The choice was eventually to be a variant of the Northrop F-5 Freedom Fighter. Influencing the choice were the low initial cost, twin engine reliability, proven serviceability, and rapid deployment features of the F-5, characteristics which filled the requirements of the new role as they were perceived at that time.

There were four basic taskings anticipated for the new aircraft. Close support for ground forces was seen as the primary role—attacking hostile targets in the proximity of the ground force with a variety of conventional weapons with the close cooperation of the ground force. For the interdiction role, the fighter would be required to attack enemy communications and transportation facilities at a distance in order to slow down their advance. Surveillance of the battle area for enemy activity and photographic and visual reconnaissance of specific points of tactical importance completed the required roles. As well, the aircraft must have an air defence capability, in order to defend itself and to protect the ground forces from enemy attack.

The operational squadrons equipped with the CF-5 would be stationed in Canada to be available for joint exercises and training with the land forces, but be capable of overseas deployment within a short time. An air-to-air refuelling capability was planned to increase the mobility

necessary for these taskings. The aircraft would be employed in close cooperation with the land forces in situations ranging from peacekeeping duties to limited conventional war. In the event of a United Nations request to provide a special land/air force to enforce the aims of the organization, the fighters would deploy to the area, being refuelled in the air from staging bases in friendly areas.

On 14 July 1965 the Canadian government announced an order for one hundred and fifteen aircraft, comprising eighty-nine single seat, designated CF-5A and twenty-six two seat aircraft designated CF-5D intended for service with Canadian forces. The Canadair designator was CL-219-1A10 for the single seat aircraft and CL-219-1A17 for the dual seat aircraft. The CF-5A aircraft were equivalent to the F-5-15 or F-5C models (as used by USAF in Vietnam), and were to be produced under licence by Canadair at their facility in Cartierville in the greater Montreal area. The government of The Netherlands placed an order for ninety NF-5A and NF-5B, later revised to seventy-five NF-5A and thirty NF-5B aircraft. Canadair designator was CL-226-1A10 for the single seat aircraft, and CL-226-1A11-5B for the two seaters. The engines, the J-85-CAN-15 for both purchases were to be built under licence by Orenda Engines Ltd., at Malton, which was producing the J-85-CAN-4040 engines for the Canadair CT114 Tutor training aircraft.

The Republic F-105D Thunderchief, the preferred choice of the RCAF to equip the tactical fighter squadrons in Mobile Command.

(A. Stachiw)

A NF-5A, serial no. K-3005, along with a pair of CF-5A aircraft, awaiting delivery outside the Canadair plant at Cartierville in February 1970.

(Canadair Ltd. Neg. No. 12964-4)

The first CF-5A, serial no. 14701, was rolled out in a ceremony held at Canadair on 6 February 1968, and the second, serial no. 14702, shortly after. Both of these aircraft were transported by Canadian Forces CC130 Hercules aircraft to Edwards AFB in California. The first, now reserialled 116701, was flown by Northrop test pilot Henri Chouteau on 3 May 1968, the flight lasting sixty-one minutes. This aircraft was written off on 3 December 1969 at Edwards AFB. The third aircraft, a CF-5D, serial no. 116801, was first flown by William Longhurst at the Canadair plant at Cartierville on August 27 with Henri Chouteau aboard.

While the aircraft were being built, the pilots that would fly the CF-5s received training at Williams AFB in Arizona. Prior to the delivery of the Canadair-built aircraft, stock Northrop F-5 aircraft, both single (serial no. 58-38421) and two seat models (serial no. 58-38445), were test flown by pilots of the Aerospace Engineering and Test Establishment (AETE) based at RCAF Uplands south of Ottawa. These aircraft, still wearing their USAF serial numbers, had rudimentary Canadian markings applied for public relations purposes.

A NF-5B, serial no. K-4002, just off the production line at Canadair Ltd.
(Canadair Ltd. Neg. No. 8907)

Canadair-built aircraft for the Canadian Forces were delivered initially to the Aeronautical Engineering and Test Establishment, located by then at Cold Lake, Alberta, including CF-5A 116702, and CF-5D 116801. Later deliveries, commencing with 116802 on 5 November 1968, were assigned to 434 "Bluenose" Tactical Fighter (Operational Training) Squadron, also located at Cold Lake. The second Squadron, 433 "Porc-Epic" Escadrille Tactique de Combat (433 "Porcupine" Tactical Fighter Squadron), based at Bagotville, Quebec received its first aircraft on 18 November 1969.

Originally intentions were to form four squadrons (some sources say six squadrons) equipped with CF-5 aircraft. However, cutbacks in defence funding and a shift in defence policy—announced by Prime Minister Trudeau on 6 April 1969 and explained in detail in the government's White Paper on Defence published in August 1970—gave priority to the defence of North America and the maintenance of Canadian sovereignty, and peacekeeping became a less important tasking for the Canadian Armed Forces. The quick-reaction photographic reconnaissance mission would now be a vital part of the general surveillance of Canadian territory, air space and sea approaches. The weapon carrying tasks of the CF-5 were to be retained for two operational squadrons earmarked for the Canadian contribution to the defence of the Northern

Flank of NATO. As a consequence, a number of CF-5 aircraft were declared surplus to operational requirement, and were placed in storage at the Air Maintenance Development Unit facility at Canadian Forces Base Trenton, and were then operated on a rotational basis.

In December 1971 the sale of sixteen single seat CF-5A, and two dual seat CF-5D aircraft was negotiated with the government of Venezuela. These aircraft were provided from existing inventory, with two new-build CF-5Ds to follow, at a price of $38 million, with support equipment and spares. The Fuerza Aerea Venezolianos had been looking for a replacement for its fleet of F-86F Sabre interceptors, and had also negotiated the purchase of sixteen Dassault Mirage interceptors from France.

In addition, to more closely satisfy the requirements of the Canadian Forces, twenty more CF-5D aircraft would be built (116827 to 116846, of which two new-build aircraft would be provided to Venezuela [116827, 116828], the remainder to be used for advanced training). The CF-5D aircraft would replace the CT133 Silver Star Mk.3 in that role. The net cost, since the CF-5D aircraft were more expensive to produce, would be $10 million extra to the Canadian government.

The Northrop Corporation then filed suit against the Government of Canada, seeking more than $17.5 million in damages and payments arising out of the production program for the CF-5 aircraft built by Canadair Ltd. under licence from Northrop. Northrop cancelled the agreement permitting CF-5 production at Canadair, although allowing completion of those aircraft already in production.

The Northrop claim sought damages arising from the sale of the twenty CF-5 aircraft to Venezuela, which Northrop claimed was in violation of the licence agreement, plus royalties and payments due to Northrop under the contract, but which had been withheld by the Canadian government. The payments and royalties had been withheld for three years, since negotiations began between the government and Canadair over production problems and increased costs experienced by the company on the program. The company had stated that its production difficulties were due to failures by Northrop to provide adequate and timely manufacturing data and assistance under the licencing agreement. Northrop dismissed the claims as unfounded. The Canadian government subsequently took the position that Northrop should reimburse it for the cost of an added payment to Canadair. However, Northrop had not been party to the settlement of that payment, and the government had refused Northrop's offer of assistance in the negotiations leading to the settlement. The matter was finally settled out of court, with the Canadian government paying Northrop $9 million.

An F-5B test and demonstration aircraft lifts off the runway at the Canadair plant.
(Canadair Ltd. Neg. No. 49889)

The prototype installation of the inflight refuelling system installed on the CF-5A fleet was first tested on aircraft 116704. Trials were undertaken using an RAF Handley Page Victor K.Mk.2 tanker aircraft. With the introduction into service of the Boeing 707-347C, designated CC137 in CF service, and the conversion of two of those aircraft as tankers, the CF-5 fleet gained a new versatility.

In 1972, two CF-5 aircraft were deployed to Europe to participate in Operation Fencer, to evaluate the use of the CF-5 in support of the defence of the Northern Flank of Europe by NATO. These aircraft were flown across the Atlantic by way of Greenland, Iceland, and Scotland to Norway. This role was eventually assigned to the Canadian Forces. In 1973, after trials in Canada, the first deployment to Europe with the aid of air-to-air refuelling took place. The CF-5s were flown across the Atlantic to Norway, refuelled enroute by the Canadian Forces Boeing CC137 tanker aircraft of 437 "Husky" Transport Squadron based at CFB Trenton. In preparation for this tasking, CF-5 aircrew underwent intensive training in air-to-air refuelling techniques. The first trans-Atlantic deployment took place on 9 June1973 when eight aircraft were flown non-stop to Andoya, Norway in exercise Long Leap I. Several weeks of operations there proved the feasability of the concept.

In September 1973 the Canadair CF116D Freedom Fighter replaced the Canadair CT133 Silver Star Mk.3 as the advanced pilot trainer of the Canadian Forces. 1 Canadian Forces Flying Training School (1 CFFTS), based at CFB Cold Lake, Alberta converted to the operation of the CF-5, and the first class graduated on the new trainer in October 1974. Initially, the students received instruction in the Basic Fighter Pilot's Course. On 1 November 1975, 419 Tactical Fighter Training Squadron was reactivated, assuming the role of advanced flying training and operational training. Pilots destined to fly the CF101B Voodoo and the CF104 Starfighter were to be given their initiation into high performance flight in the CF-5, as was previously done by 434 TACF(OT) Squadron. The curriculum would be further expanded in the years to follow. When the CF-18 Hornet was chosen to replace the CF101 Voodoo and CF104 Starfighter fleets, the CF-5 was used as Fighter Lead In Trainer (FLIT) for the new aircraft.

When 433e ETAC took part in exercises at the US Marine Corp Air Combat Maneuvering Range at Yuma, Arizona, the pilots were highly enthusiastic. They felt that their level of ACM experience was greatly enhanced. During debriefings, the pilots witnessed their own performance in relation to the others, and experience quickly grew as pilots became increasingly aware of tactics, missile envelope parameters, and the limitations of themselves and their aircraft. Experience gained from ACMR would undoubtedly lower losses to an enemy in air-to-air combat. With the establishment of the Air Combat Maneuvering Range at Cold Lake, the CF-5 aircraft were employed in using this asset to enhance the capabilities of the pilots undergoing training. Training value was maximized while minimizing risk to the pilots and equipment by virtue of the unique monitoring capability of the system. Air-to-air combat and air-to-ground weapon delivery could be accurately simulated for aircraft in varying roles without the inherent risks and cost of using actual weapons. It brought a level of training that was not previously attainable.

Emphasis on offensive air support as a primary role for the Canadian Forces commitment to the defence of the Northern Flank of Europe gained prominence in the 1980s. In March 1980 the system of tactical evaluations (Tac Evals) was introduced, giving opportunity for the units to test operational capabilities and to establish priorities in the tactical support role. On 15 July 1982 Fighter Group was created, ending the last direct link between the CF-5 operational squadrons and 10 Tactical Air Group and Mobile Command. The role of operational tactical fighter was now assigned to the two squadrons, 434 "Bluenose" Tactical Fighter Squadron, at CFB Cold Lake, and 433 "Porc-Epic" Escadrille Tactique de Combat (433 "Porcupine" Tactical Fighter Squadron), based at CFB Bagotville, Quebec. On 19 April 1986, a ceremony was held at Bagotville marking the end of CF-5 Freedom Fighter operations. At that time 433 ETAC had fully converted to the CF188 Hornet fighter. The end of tactical fighter operations by 434 TAC(F) Squadron took place when the unit was disbanded in June 1988 at CFB Chatham.

A contract was issued in 1987 to Bristol Aerospace Ltd., located at Winnipeg International Airport, to rebuild fifty-eight aircraft (thirty-three CF-5A and twenty-three CF-5D), later revised to thirty-six (thirteen CF-5A and twenty-three CF-5D). A second program was initiated in 1990 to upgrade the avionics package in forty-four aircraft (eleven CF-5a and thirty-three CF-5D). The refurbished aircraft were employed as lead-in trainers for the CF-18 Hornet, in effect becoming flying simulators.

The CF-5 remained in service with 419 F(T) Squadron as an advanced fighter trainer until, in 1995, the Department of National Defence initiated a twenty-five percent cutback in the strength of Fighter Group. As a result, a substantial number of CF-18 Hornet aircraft were placed in storage. To prevent further cuts in the CF-18 fleet, the CF-5 fleet was withdrawn from the active inventory on 31 March 1995, declared surplus and put up for disposal. A sale was negotiated with the government of Botswana for the sale of a total of sixteen aircraft (see Table 2-1, CF-5 Fleet Statistics), all having had the updates. The remaining aircraft are at the time of writing for sale, with negotiations underway to potential customers. Negotiations with the U.S. Navy for use of the upgraded aircraft in the Top Gun Program did not result in further sales, although there are ongoing negotiations with the Greek government for the use of the CF-5 as Fighter Lead In Trainer for their F-16 fighter fleet.

The CF-5 fleet was in service with the Canadian Forces for some twenty-six years, and would have soldiered on for many more years had there not been cutbacks in government funding. During that time it was assigned different roles with changes in defence policy, and served well in any role it was given. Although there was no shortage of controversy associated with the service of the Freedom Fighter in the Canadian Forces, it was well regarded by the units that were equipped with the aircraft, and always a crowd pleaser when it performed for the public at airshows across the country. The spirited performance of this diminutive fighter will remain as a fond memory to those who now view the aircraft on display at several museums across Canada.

CF-5 FLEET STATISTICS

S/N	C/N	TOS	Del Date	SOS	Sub S/N	Comments
14701/116701	1001	68.2.8	68.2.7	70.5.19		W/O Cat.A 69.12.3 AETE Edwards AFB
116702x	1002	68.2.7	68.5.2			Prototype reconnaissance nose instl. ATESS
116703x	1003	69.1.14	69.1.23			ATESS
116704x	1004	71.1.16	71.3.3			Prototype aerial refueling instl. ATESS
116705*	1005	69.10.22	A69.11.2			Sold to Botswana
116706	1006	69.10.22	69.10.22	80.11.3		W/O Cat.A 79.12.13 433e ETAC Bagotville
116707*	1007	69.10.22	69.10.21			Prototype avionics update, not rewired
116708	1008	69.11.10	69.11.7	70.9.30		W/O Cat.A 70.8.21 433e ETAC Bagotville
116709x	1009	70.1.27	70.4.28			ATESS
116710	1010	70.4.7	70.8.5			W/O Cat.A
116711	1011	70.5.22	70.5.27	74.7.10		W/O Cat.A 74.1.3 433e ETAC Bagotville
116712x	1012	70.4.7	70.4.7			ATESS
116713x	1013	69.10.22	69.12.11			ATESS
116714x	1014	69.10.22	69.12.12			ATESS
116715	1015	69.12.24	70.1.20			Display 1 Canadian Division, Kingston, ON
116716*	1016	69.12.24	70.1.31			Sold to Botswana
116717x	1017	69.10.22	69.12.30			ATESS
116718	1018	70.1.15	69.12.24	71.5.4		W/O Cat.A 70.8.21 433e ETAC Bagotville
116719*	1019	69.12.24	70.2.2	96.		Sold to Botswana
116720	1020	69.12.24	69.12.24	88.5.5		W/O Cat.A 87.11.12 434 TAC(F) Chatham
116721	1021	69.10.22	69.12.29			Display at RCAF Memorial Museum, CFB Trenton
116722	1022	70.1.12	70.1.12	72.3.13		W/O Cat.A 71.9.20 433e ETAC Bagotville
116723*	1023	69.12.24	70.1.19	96.		Sold to Botswana
116724	1024	69.12.24	70.1.22			Display Canadian Air Land Sea Museum
116725	1025	69.12.24	69.12.24	88.5.26		CFB Borden ABDR
116726	1026	70.1.27	70.4.28			Canadian Air Land Sea Museum
116727*	1027	70.1.27	70.4.28	96.		Sold to Botswana

S/N	C/N	TOS	Del Date	SOS	Sub S/N	Comments
116728	1028	70.4.7	70.4.7	80.2.20		W/O Cat.A 79.7.11 433e ETA Cold Lake
116729#	1029	70.1.22	70.1.27	88.5.26		DADTT Canadair
116730	1030	70.4.7	70.1.30			Display MMM Campbelford, ON
116731	1031	70.7.10	70.4.7	77.9.26		W/O Cat.A 77.5.6 433e ETAC Bagotville
116732*	1032	70.4.7	70.6.4	96.		Sold to Botswana
116733	1033	70.4.7	70.4.7	91.8.9		Display Bagotville, QC
116734*	1034	70.1.27	70.4.15	96.		Sold to Botswana
116735	1035	70.8.24	70.8.24	84.1.16		W/O Cat.A 81.2.26 433e ETAC Bagotville
116736	1036	70.8.24	70.8.24	88.11.10		Display Cold Lake
116737	1037	70.4.7	70.4.7	88.5.26		CFB Borden ABDR
116738	1038	70.4.7	70.4.15			Display MMM Campbelford, ON
116739	1039	70.4.7	70.4.9			Display Trenton Holiday Inn
116740	1040	71.1.16	71.2.5			Display Kamloops, BC
116741	1041	70.8.5	71.2.11	76.10.12		W/O Cat.A 76.3.2 AETE Cold Lake
116742	1042	70.10.13	70.10.22	94.4.14		Flight Procedures Trainer Sold to Botswana
116743	1043	70.4.7	70.11.26			Display Canadian Air Land Sea Museum
116744	1044	70.4.7	70.11.29	92.4.13		CFB borden ABDR
116745	1045	70.9.5	70.11.17	88.5.26		Reduced to spares
116746	1046	70.6.8	70.6.16	98.3.16		DisplayToronto Air Museum Downsview, ON
116747	1047	70.4.7	70.7.10	92.3.24		Display Canadian Air Land Sea Museum
116748	1048	70.4.7	70.8.14	98.3.27		Display Atlantic Canada Aviation Museum, Halifax, NS
116749	1049	70.4.7	70.6.29		A887	Display Heritage Air Park Winnipeg, MB
116750	1050	70.9.15	70.9.21			ATESS
116751x	1051	70.4.7	70.7.16			ATESS
116752	1052	70.9.21	70.9.21			W/O Cat.A 70.6.16 Canadair Ltd. Montreal, QC
116753	1053	70.4.7	70.7.10			Display Cold Lake, AB
116754*	1054	70.4.7	70.7.10	96.		Sold to Botswana
116755	1055	70.8.17	70.8.14	77.10.7		W/O Cat.A 77.6.7 419 F(T) Sqn Cold Lake
116756	1056	70.10.21	70.10.19	74.11.27		W/O Cat.A 74.5.12 433eetac Cold Lake
116757	1057	70.4.7	70.8.14	89.5.8		Display Canadian Warplane Heritage Museum, Hamilton, ON
116758x	1058	70.8.20	70.12.4			ATESS
116759	1059	70.9.15	70.9.4			W/O Cat.A
116760	1060	70.12.2	70.11.30	77.4.22		W/O Cat.A 76.5.2 419 F(T) Sqn Cold Lake
116761	1061	70.8.20	70.12.4	83.10.18		W/O Cat.A 79.2.12 419 F(T) Sqn Cold Lake
116762	1062	70.12/16	70.12.18	88.5.26		CFB Borden ABDR
116763	1063	70.8.20	70.12.4	97.9.29		Display National Aviation Museum Ottawa, ON
116764*	1064	70.8.28	70.12.3	96.		Sold to Botswana
116765*	1065	70.4.7	70.11.30	96.		Sold to Botswana
116766	1066	70.12.16	70.12.15			CFB Borden ABDR
116767	1067	71.1.16	71.1.26	72.2.3	6719	To Venezuela
116768*	1068	70.8.20	70.12.9			ATESS
116769	1069	70.12.16	70.12.21		845B	Display CFB Borden

S/N	C/N	TOS	Del Date	SOS	Sub S/N	Comments
116770	1070	70.12.29	70.12.22	7	8.4.13	W/O Cat.A 77.8.10 433e ETAC Bagotville
116771	1071	70.8.20	70.12.30	83.1.25		W/O Cat.A 83.1.20 434 TAC(F) Sqn Chatham
116772	1072	70.8.20	70.12.29			Display MMM Campbelford, ON
116773	1073	70.8.20	70.12.30	72.5.26	7200	To Venezuela
116774	1074	70.8.28	71.3.10	72.2.3	6539	To Venezuela
116775	1075	71.6.29	71.6.29	72.3.29	9124	To Venezuela
116776	1076	71.1.20	71.1.20	72.5.26	6323	To Venezuela
116777	1077	71.1.13	71.1.7	72.3.29	6018	To Venezuela
116778	1078	71.1.29	71.1.18	72.3.29	5276	To Venezuela
116779	1079	71.1.19	71.1.29	72.5.26	3318	To Venezuela
116780	1080	71.1.29	71.1.26	72.3.29	3274	To Venezuela
116781	1081	71.1.29	71.1.28	72.3.29	2950	To Venezuela
116782	1082	71.2.12	70.8.20	72.3.29	9538	To Venezuela
116783	1083	71.2.11	71.2.5	72.3.29	9456	To Venezuela
116784*	1084	71.2.1	71.2.26	96.		Sold to Botswana
116785	1085	71.2.1	71.3.1	89.5.8		CFB Borden ABDR
116786	1086	71.3.24	71.3.19	72.3.29	9348	To Venezuela
116787	1087	71.6.15	71.6.15	72.5.26	8792	To Venezuela
116788	1088	71.4.6	71.1.6	72.5.26	9215	To Venezuela
116789	1089	71.9.21	71.9.16	72.5.26	8707	To Venezuela
116801*	2001	68.10.3	68.10.29	96.		Sold to Botswana
116802*	2002	68.10.18	68.11.5	96.		Sold to Botswana
116803	2003	68.12.3	68.12.4	72.2.11	1269	To Venezuela
116804	2004	68.12.10	68.12.5	69.8.14		W/O Cat.B 69.3 434 TACF(OT) Sqn Cold Lake
116805*	2005	68.12.9	69.1.10			ATESS
116806x	2006	68.12.9	69.1.9			ATESS
116807*	2007	68.12.9	69.1.22			ATESS
116808	2008	69.2.4	69.1.30	72.2.11	2327	To Venezuela
116809#	2009	68.12.9	69.3.28			ATESS
116810x	2010	68.12.9	69.3.10			ATESS
116811*	2011	68.12.9	69.3.10	96.		Sold to Botswana
116812*	2012	68.12.9	69.4.25			ATESS
116813#	2013	68.12.9	69.4.15			ATESS
116814#	2014	68.12.9	69.5.23			ATESS
116815#	2015	68.12.9	69.5.24			ATESS
116816	2016	68.12.9	69.6.16	84.1.16		W/O Cat.A 83.3.7
116817	2017	68.12.9	69.6.16	84.2.23		W/O Cat.A 83.12.22 419 F(T) Sqn Westover AFB
116818*	2018	69.8.5	69.8.28			ATESS
116819#	2019	68.12.9	69.7.3	93.12.1		W/O Cat.A 92.1.10 419 F(T) Sqn
116820*	2020	69.6.18	69.6.26			ATESS
116821*	2021	68.12.9	69.8.22			ATESS
116822#	2022	69.8.5	69.8.22			ATESS
116823*	2023	68.12.9	69.7.17			ATESS
116824*	2024	69.8.5	69.8.22			ATESS

S/N	C/N	TOS	Del Date	SOS	Sub S/N	Comments
116825	2025	69.9.8	69.9.23	00.		Sold to Intertrade, California
116826#	2026	69.8.5	69.10.15			ATESS
116827	2027	73.12.6	73.12.6	73.12.6	2985	To Venezuela
116828	2028	74.1.2	74.1.2	74.1.2	5681	To Venezuela
116829*	2029	74.1.9	74.2.4	96.		Sold to Botswana
116830*	2030	74.1.9	74.2.11	96.		Sold to Botswana
116831*	2031	74.1.9	74.2.27			ATESS
116832x	2032	74.1.9	74.4.22			ATESS
116833*	2033	74.1.9	74.3.25			Demonstration Acft - Bristol Aerospace
116834#	2034	74.1.9	74.4.10			ATESS
116835*	2035	74.1.9	74.6.5			ATESS
116836*	2036	74.1.9	74.7.9			ATESS
116837*	2037	74.1.9	74.5.23			ATESS
116838#	2038	74.1.9	74.6.19			ATESS
116839*	2039	74.1.9	74.6.20			Demonstration Acft - Bristol Aerospace
116840*	2040	74.1.9	74.8.13			ATESS
116841*	2041	74.1.9	74.7.11			Not rewired. ATESS
116842	2042	74.1.9	74.9.30	88.11.10		W/O Cat.A 88.9. 419 F(T) Sqn
116843#	2043	74.1.9	74.9.23			ATESS
116844	2044	74.1.9	74.1.10	84.1.16		W/O Cat.A 82.4.30 419 F(T) Sqn Cold Lake
116845*	2045	74.1.9	74.12.23			ATESS
116846*	2046	74.1.9	75.1.31			ATESS

ABDR	Aircraft Battle Damage Repair
W/O	Written Off
*	Received full AUP upgrade
#	Received partial upgrade (DLIR)
x	Unmodified
ATESS	Storage awaiting disposal

Note: After unification of the Canadian Armed Forces was initiated in 1965, the RCAF system of aircraft type designation and serial numbering was replaced in 1972 by a CTS Control Number (Chief of Technical Services), which contained, as the prefix, the numerical part of the CTS control number, followed by a sequential tail number. In this system, the CF-5 was assigned the designator CF116 Freedom Fighter, while CF-5 Freedom Fighter remained the popular name.

In the CF-5 fleet, the single seat CF-5A aircraft were assigned the serial range 116701 to 116789. The first two aircraft were initially assigned the serials 14701 and 14702. The two seat CF-5D aircraft received the serial range 116801 to 116826, and with the further purchase of two seat aircraft, 116827 to 116846.

CF-5 FREEDOM FIGHTER SALE TO VENEZUELA

Operation Canamigo, the sale of twenty CF-5 (sixteen single seat CF-5A, serial numbers 116767, 116773 to 116783 incl., and 116786 to 116789 incl.; and four dual seat CF-5D aircraft, serial numbers 116803, 116808, 116827, 116828) was negotiated in December 1969 with the government of Venezuela. The sales agreement included the training of pilots and ground crew of the Fuerza Aerea Venezolianos in Canada, and the provision of a team of Canadian advisers to instruct and organize a training program in Venezuela. Most of the advisory team members were selected from 434 TACF(OT) Sqn at CFB Cold Lake, with one instructor pilot and one supply technician being provided by 433e ETAC, CFB Bagotville. The Detachment, dubbed "Mission Canadiense" consisted of three instructor pilots and twelve maintenance supervisors and technicians.

The Canadian Forces were also responsible for the delivery of the aircraft. The aircraft, selected from operational reserve, were prepared by the Aircraft Maintenance and Development Unit (AMDU) at CFB Trenton

A lineup of grounded VF-5A aircraft at Barquisimeto, October 1990, in short term storage pending financing for upgrades. The closest aircraft, serial number 6018, is former CF-5A 116777.

(Peter R. Foster)

for delivery. These aircraft were ferried in three groups by pilots from 433e ETAC and 434 TACF(OT) squadrons. Each group was supported by a VAF C-130 Hercules aircraft which transported the accompanying groundcrew and a ferry maintenance kit. The delivery flights took place between February and June 1972, after the aircraft had been refinished in Venezuelan markings by Field Aviation at CFB Trenton. The first leg of the trip was from CFB Trenton to Homestead AFB, Florida, with a refueling stop at Myrtle Beach, South Carolina. The second leg, of approximately 1,000 miles, was from Homestead to San Juan, Puerto Rico, and the final leg from Puerto Rico to El Libertador Base on the eastern shore of Lake Valencia, approximately forty miles southwest of Caracas, the capital city of Venezuela. Captain Hank Morris of 433e ETAC was one of the Canadian advisers that accompanied each flight. He made the necessary radio calls in Spanish, and provided interpretation for other members of the flight.

Captain Morris and two other pilots and twelve ground crew had spent the previous six months in Venezuela training the VAF personnel in the flying and maintenance of the aircraft. A total of ten pilots and thirty-five technicians were trained on the CF-5 and its support systems, three pilots having been trained at Cold Lake on the six month course the previous winter.

The aircraft, designated VF-5A and VF-5D in FAV service, were allocated to Grupo de Caza No. 11 "Diabolos", based at Barquisimeto, forming the equipment of Esquadron de Caza No.34 and No.35. Two single seat aircraft were later converted to RVF-5A reconnaissance configuration. By May 1990 seven aircraft had been lost, and the remainder grounded by fatigue problems. Budgetary restraints forced the retirement of the surviving aircraft and the entire fleet was placed in storage.

In June 1990 a contract was signed with Singapore Aerospace to upgrade the fleet with GPS equipment and inflight refueling probes. This work was carried out in Venezuela with assistance by technicians from the contractor. The thirteen surviving VF-5A and single VF-5B were sent to Singapore Aerospace for refurbishment, with a single VF-5A and VF-5B being returned by May of 1993, and the remainder by May 1994. As well, late in 1990 seven surplus aircraft (6 NF-5B and one NF-5A) were obtained from the Netherlands, all of which were delivered by 1993.

In November 1992 elements of the FAV participated in an unsuccessful coup against the Government. Because of the dispersal of the VF-5s due to the ongoing upgrade program, these aircraft did not play a significant part in the fighting, although one was scrambled to defend the Barquisimeto Air Base. Three VF-5 aircraft were destroyed on the ground by raiding Mirage and Bronco aircraft of the rebel force.

Esquadron de Caza No.36, as part of Grupo Aereo de Caza No.12 based at Barquisimeto, still operate the surviving eight VF-5A, three NF-5B, and single VF-5D aircraft. However, it is no longer considered operational, and functions as a training group in support of the Mirage fighters of Grupo 11 and F-16 fighters of Grupo 16.

THE NF-5 FREEDOM FIGHTER FOR THE NETHERLANDS

In 1966 the Koninklijke Luchtmacht (Royal Netherlands Air Force) sought a replacement for its fleet of Republic F-84F Thunderstreak tactical fighter aircraft. Originally, coproduction of the F-5 with Belgium had been planned, but the Belgians opted for the Dassault Mirage F.5 instead. Although there were misgivings with the F-5, the Canadair-produced aircraft had the improvements embodied which had been required. As well, a significant offset program to the Dutch aerospace companies, Fokker and Avio Diepen, to produce fuselage and tail assemblies for the Dutch order as well as for the Canadian aircraft resulted in the Netherlands government placing an order with Canadair on 1 February 1967, rather than having them built in Holland.

The fighters received the designation NF-5A for the single seat aircraft (ninety examples designated Canadair CL-226-1A10), and NF-5B for the two seaters (thirty examples designated Canadair CL-226-1A11). The first NF-5A, serial no. K-3001, was rolled out on 5 March 1969,

NF-5A serial no. K-3030 in service with 313 Squadron of the Royal Netherlands Air Force.
(Robert Bryden)

first flown by William Longhurst on 24 March and handed over to the Netherlands on 7 October. The first NF-5B, serial K-4001, was flown on 7 July 1969, piloted by S. Grossman. These two aircraft were flown to Edwards AFB for flight testing, while the remainder were test flown in Canada. Deliveries of the aircraft were completed when an NF-5A, serial number K-3075 was handed over on 10 March 1972.

The Dutch NF-5s were basically the same as the CF-5, incorporating all the improvements found in that version of the F-5. In addition, NF-5 aircraft featured manoeuvering flap gear in a strengthened wing assembly to better enable the aircraft to perform high speed combat manoeuvers, significantly decreasing the combat turn radius. The internal fuel capacity was increased, and the stronger wing allowed increased external fuel capacity and/or ordinance, and provision was made for ejector bomb racks.

A good part of the avionics as fitted to the CF-5 were deleted from the NF-5 fleet. The NF-5 had the standard Northrop non-computing gunsight, and the Sperry gyro heading and reference system was replaced by a Bendix attitude and heading reference system. A Canadian Marconi Type 688 Doppler navigation system and Type 703 navigation system and rolling map display was installed, as was an attitude heading and reference system, emergency UHF radio, and a radio altimeter. Upgrades were incorporated throughout the service life of the NF-5 fleet. The canopies were improved, new avionics were incorporated, including a radar warning receiver, and ALE-40 chaff and flare dispensers were installed on the rear fuselage. The wingtip fuel tanks were replaced by AIM-9 Sidewinder launching rails on some aircraft.

The aircraft were ferried to the Netherlands in an operation named Project Hi-Flite, the first of which took place in November 1969. Several ways of delivery were considered including by surface ship, airlift, and commercial contract ferrying. When the USAF 2nd Aircraft Delivery Group agreed to support the transatlantic ferry flights, the RNAF decided to perform the operation. The group prepared the flight logs for the NF-5 pilots, and provided weather and operational briefings enroute. Two Lockheed C-130 Hercules airborne navigation stations, nicknamed Duck Butts, were used to support the ferry flights. These aircraft, equipped with

UHF and direction finding radio and radar, circled at 25,000 ft. at the midpoint of each overwater leg, providing navigation fixes and air-sea rescue equipment and paramedics in the event of any crash landing or ejection at sea.

The aircraft were first accepted at the Canadair plant at Cartierville from where they were flown to CFB Bagotville, where an RNAF technical team was stationed to service the aircraft. After two weeks of preparation and two to four shakedown flights, a flight of four aircraft would depart Bagotville in the afternoon for Goose Bay, in dual formation, with a twenty to thirty-minute separation. The aircraft were not equipped for inflight refueling, and were flown in the lightest possible configuration to enable flying over most of the weather, reducing pilot fatigue. The flights were made in four stages. The first, Goose Bay to Sondrestrom, Greenland, was the longest leg of the journey, and the aircraft would arrive at Sondrestrom with maximum thirty minutes of fuel remaining. The pilots had to be sure of the weather before departing Goose Bay since there was no alternate field within reach. From there they flew to Keflavik, Iceland, then to Lossiemouth, Scotland, and finally, to Twenthe, in the Netherlands.

The NF-5 aircraft were assigned to four squadrons. The first aircraft went to 315 Squadron based at Twenthe, which became Omscholingsvlucht or Operational Conversion Unit (OCU), training pilots for the other squadrons as they came on line. They were the first to transition to the F-16 Fighting Falcon in 1986. No. 314 Squadron, an attack squadron equipped primarily with NF-5A, which was based at Eindhoven, transitioned to the F-16 in 1990. No. 313 Squadron, also based at Twenthe, became an advanced training unit and was equipped with the NF-5B only. The unit transitioned to the F-16 in 1987, and No.316 Squadron, also an attack squadron equipped with NF-5A, was based at Gilze-Rijen, and transitioned to the F-16 in 1991. The NF-5 Freedom Fighters stood down on 1 May 1991 when No. 316 Squadron completed its conversion to F-16. Some of the surplus NF-5 aircraft went to Turkey (sixty) and Greece (eleven) under NATO Agreement, and seven were purchased by Venezuela, as previously mentioned. The remaining surviving aircraft are on display in museums or were transferred to technical schools in the Netherlands.

CHAPTER THREE

Aircraft Descriptions and Drawings

CF-5A serial no. 116726 on a test flight over the Laurentian Mountains north of Montreal. Note the pristine finish of the aircraft.

(Canadair Ltd, Neg. No. 12055-3)

Front view of CF-5A aircraft, 116726. Note the characteristic "peanut" shape of the auxiliary fuel tanks mounted on the wing tips, and the muzzles of the 20mm cannon in the aircraft nose.

(A. Stachiw)

CANADAIR CF-5A FREEDOM FIGHTER

Canadair designator CL-219-1A10, CTS Control Number CF116A

Description: Single seat air superiority, strike / ground support and reconnaissance, and advanced operational training fighter aircraft, of all metal construction, with provision for inflight refueling.

Powerplant: Two General Electric J-85 CAN-15 (Orenda-built) turbojet engines
2820 lbs. (1281 kg.) thrust, 2925 lbs. (1329.5 kg.) thrust military power
4300 lb. (1950 kg) thrust, with afterburning

Dimensions:
- Wingspan with tip tanks 25.8ft (7.85m)
- Height 13.2 ft (4.01m)
- Length 47.2 ft (14.38m)
- Wing Area 174 ft2 (16.16m2)

Weights: CF-5A Empty 9607 lbs. (4387 kg.)
CF-5AR Empty 9748 lbs. (4431 kg.)
CF-5A Takeoff weight without external stores 14,150 lbs. (6418 kg.)
CF-5AR Takeoff weight without external stores 14,291 lbs. (6495.9 kg.)
CF-5A Maximum takeoff weight 20,390 lbs. (9249 kg.)
CF-5AR Maximum takeoff weight 20,521 lbs. (9327.7 kg.)

Performance: Max speed sea level at 11,630 lbs. (5276 kg.) in clean configuration, M 1.04
Max speed at 36,000 ft. (10,970 m) in clean configuration, M 1.48
Takeoff distance at 13,400 lbs. (6.078 kg.) 1900 ft. (579m)
Max rate of climb 33,000 ft/min (10,058 m/min)

Armament: Two internally mounted M39 20mm cannon plus a variety of combinations of externally mounted ordnance and/or externally mounted fuel tanks *(see Chapter 6)*. A lead computing Ferranti ISIS gyro optical gunsight was installed.

Three-quarter front port side view of CF-5A aircraft, 116726. The "Porc-Epic" insignia on the disc just aft of the engine air intake identifies the aircraft as being in service with 433e ETAC.

(A. Stachiw)

Port side view of CF-5A aircraft, 116726. This view accentuates the sleek appearance of the diminutive fighter.

(A. Stachiw)

Three-quarter rear port side view of CF-5A aircraft 116726. Note the housing for the braking parachute just above the twin exhaust tubes of the jet engines.

(A. Stachiw)

Rear view of CF-5A aircraft 116726.

(A. Stachiw)

The structure of the CF-5A aircraft is broken down into small units for manufacture and ease of replacement in the event of damage. Spares for both single and two seat models are eighty percent interchangeable aft of the canted bulkhead behind the cockpit.

The forward fuselage contains the fire control and electronic equipment, nose gear, communications and navigation equipment, and the cockpit, ejection seat and controls. The upper longerons serve as the cockpit rails and support the canopy. A strengthened cockpit windscreen and canopy offered greater protection against bird strikes, anti-icing equipment was improved, and additional armour protection was provided. The windscreen is a one piece curved panel providing an unobstructed view forward, and is hinged at its forward end to provide easy access to the rear of the instrument panel. The one piece canopy is raised and lowered manually by a lever on the right inside wall of the cockpit, saving weight and maintenance time. External jettison controls are provided on both sides of the aircraft.

In the CF-5AR configuration, an optional quick change photo reconnaissance nose is fitted. The CCS-1 (Camera Control System 1) module, which was externally identical to the nose of the Northrop RF-5A variant, housed three 70mm Vinten Model 547 cameras in a variety of configurations. The installation, which necessitates minor changes to the instrument panel configuration (see Illustrations on pages 44 and 45), was tested on aircraft 116702. An inflight refueling probe, tested on CF-5AR 116704, was later to become a standard installation on all single seat aircraft. This installation is mounted on the starboard side of the forward fuselage, as opposed to being installed on the port side as in the case of the USAF aircraft that were equipped for operations in Vietnam.

Reconnaissance nose CCS-1 module, port side, of CF-5AR 116748.

(A. Stachiw)

Reconnaissance nose CCS-1 module, starboard side, of CF-5AR 116748. Note the air refuelling probe mounted on the fuselage side under the cockpit canopy.

(A. Stachiw)

The mid section of the fuselage is the largest single subassembly, containing the wing attachments, fuel tanks, and engine air intake ducts. The construction consists of four longerons, bulkheads and a floor for the fuel tank compartment. The construction of the vertical fin is integral with the main fuselage. This allows maintenance of the engines by removal of the easily handled aft fuselage and tailplane.

The forward end of the aft fuselage is of stiff construction to take the loads imposed by the tailplane through the canted fuselage joint. Aft it is composed of very light titanium frames covered externally with magnesium skin. Drag chute loads are taken forward and down to the main structure. The drag chute compartment structure is also of magnesium construction.

The empennage consists of vertical fin and rudder, and the all flying horizontal stabilator. The stabilator has a single spar attached to a steel torque tube. The entire chord, which is of honeycomb construction, serves as a torque box. The limits of travel are 17 degrees nose down and 8 degrees nose up. The vertical fin has a single canted spar attached to the main engine bulkhead and has integrally stiffened skin. The rudder is hinged to the fin's shear web, and is of honeycomb construction. With landing gear down it has a maximum travel of plus or minus 30 degrees, but inflight travel is restricted to plus or minus 6 degrees to avoid large structural loads on the vertical fin.

A two position nose landing gear, which increased the angle of attack by three degrees, was incorporated on the CF-5A, reducing takeoff distance by some twenty-five percent with heavy loads. Conventional air/oil struts are used in the landing gear. The nose gear retracts forward and is equipped with a 12-ply 18 x 6.5-8 tubeless tire. It has a combined shimmy damper and steering unit and has a travel of plus or minus 50 degrees.

Two position nose landing gear, and 125 Imperial Gallon fuel tank mounted on centre fuselage pylon.
(A. Stachiw)

The wide track main landing gear retracts inwards, with the wheels housed in the flat undersurface of the fuselage aft of the main spar of the wing. Each shock strut carries a wheel with inboard brake and 16-ply 22 x 8.5-11 tubeless tire. The independent braking system has its own reservoir and is of the single manual pressure generating type, rather than being power assisted. Both nose and main landing gear units have a manual release system, allowing them to fall free and lock down in the event of the failure of the utility hydraulic system. Barrier arrestor gear is mounted under rear centre fuselage to stop the aircraft in the event of a landing overrun.

Jettisonable underwing pylons were installed on the CF-5A and CF-5D, on which a variety of ordnance and/or jettisonable fuel tanks could be mounted (see Chapter 6).

Electro-illuminescent formation lights were installed on the CF-5 aircraft for night flying operations.

Main landing gear, and landing gear doors port side. The speed brake is mounted under the fuselage centre section aft of the main gear.

(A. Stachiw)

Barrier arrestor gear mounted under aft centre fuselage of CF-5A. Note the louvered engine inlet doors on the side of the rear fuselage (both sides) above the wing trailing edge to provide greater airflow to the engines for takeoff.

(Canadair Ltd. Neg. No. 12965A-10)

The General Electric J-85CAN-15 engine, two of which powered both CF-5A and CF-5D aircraft, were built under licence by Orenda Engines Ltd. at Malton. The higher powered engine variant, producing 4300 lb. static thrust with afterburning, conferred improved performance to the CF-5 aircraft as compared with the original F-5A. The engine air intake ducts were redesigned to accommodate the increased air requirement of the higher powered engines. Also featured were louvered engine inlet doors on each side of the rear fuselage to provide greater airflow to the engines for takeoff, and retractable air intake screens, to protect against the ingestion of debris when operating from unprepared surfaces.

The engines weigh approximately 525 lbs. (237.5 kg.) and are 21 inches (53 cm.) in diameter, and 104 inches (264.2 cm.) overall length including the afterburner. The engines are mounted on an overhead track and a simple two point mount in the mid fuselage. The engine accessory package, containing the hydraulic pump and electrical generator, is mounted on the airframe and driven by a driveshaft through universal joints. The engine bay is cooled by a series of static bleed ports just forward of the compressor entry while the engine itself is cooled by air bled from the main intake ducts.

Prototype formation light installations, CF-5A 116709. Clockwise from top left: forward fuselage; vertical stabilizer; aft fuselage and tip tank.

(S. Sauve)

General Electric J-85 CAN-15 Turbojet on dolly. Two were installed in both CF-5A and CF-5D aircraft.
(A. Stachiw)

General Electric J-85 CAN-15 Turbojet Engine
Rebuild Kit, TLD 1180. *(A. Stachiw)*

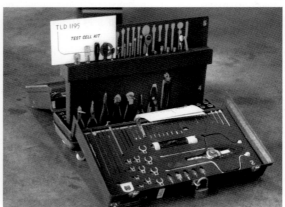

General Electric J-85 CAN-15 Turbojet Engine
Test Cell Kit, TLD 1195. *(A. Stachiw)*

For the fuel system, there are separate systems for each engine, connected by a cross-feed valve. No fuel is carried in the wing. The left circuit is fed by two dorsal cells and a forward cell, while the right hand is fed by the centre and aft cell. Both forward and aft cells incorporate an inverted flight cell, designed to supply the engines in all flight attitudes. Single point refuelling permits pressure fuelling of all tanks simultaneously, while there is provision to fuel each tank separately. Total capacity is approximately 500 Imperial Gallons. All cells are of bladder type construction, each having an AC driven booster pump, but gravity feed is possible in an emergency.

In the CF-5 aircraft, the electrical generating capacity was increased by eighty-seven percent over the F-5A. The electrical system is three-phase 115/200V AC type driving the booster pumps, fuel valves, trimming devices, flaps, air conditioning and pressurization equipment. The two generators are driven from a separate gearbox provided at the forward face of each engine so that full electrical power is available in the event of failure of either engine. An external ground power receptacle is installed.

The hydraulic system features two completely independent power systems, the flight control system and the utility hydraulic system. Each is of the pressurized closed centre type, with a pressurized reservoir. The flight control system is powered by a pump driven by the right hand engine, and the utility system by the left hand engine, both operating at all times. Under normal operation, each system supplies half the force required for control surface movement. In the event of failure of either system, the other is capable of controlling the aircraft in normal flight, the transfer being automatic, without pilot action or crossover power, each system having independent distribution. The utility system also serves the landing gear and landing gear doors, speedbrakes, stability augmentors, and nosewheel steering. No ram air turbine is installed in the event of complete engine failure. The windmilling engines provide sufficient hydraulic and electrical power to maintain control down to and including the landing. Landing can also be made on one aileron.

Full power controls are provided for the ailerons, stabilator and rudder. The ailerons each have a dual hydraulic actuator, controlled by a cable system from the control stick. The rudder pedals are connected by cables and pushrods to servos on dual actuators. In order to avoid large loads on the vertical stabilizer during yaw manoeuvres, pedal travel is restricted when the landing gear is retracted. A subsystem provides Dutch roll damping and

interconnection between rudder and ailerons compensates for non-linear inertia forces during roll manoeuvres and provides rudder trim authority.

A spring and bob weight provide the stick forces and centering action for the horizontal stabilator which is powered by two hydraulic actuators. One cylinder of each actuator is powered by the flight control hydraulic system, the other by the utility system. Controls from the stick to the servo valves are duplicated, and pitch damping is provided. Free play is eliminated by preloading the actuators through the torque tube.

Automatic trim change takes place when the flaps are raised or lowered, and a push button control allows the pilot to select the correct stabilator angle for takeoff with hands off the stick. Trim is provided for all three control surfaces, operation of the switches on the stick grip controlling the stabilator and ailerons, while a potentiometer on the left console trims the rudder. Movement of the trailing edge flaps also actuates the leading edge flaps, both systems being electrically driven.

The speed brakes are located under the centre fuselage, and can be depressed to any angle up to 46 degrees. Each is actuated by its own hydraulic jack, but both are controlled by a single switch on the right hand power lever.

The CF-5 aircraft were equipped with an upgraded UHF/DF Sperry navigation system. In addition, all communication equipment was upgraded compared to the stock F-5 aircraft. The installations included a central air data computer, Gyro Heading Reference System, AN/ARC-51B UHF communications radio, TACAN, IFF, and a lead-computing Ferranti ISIS (AWQ-501) gyro-optical gunsight was provided.

The ease of maintenance is a feature of the aircraft design. There are 111 access panels on the fuselage alone, and all operational fittings and connections can be reached with ease. Components likely to require frequent replacement are located in the most accessible positions, and all others can be tested in place. Very little ground support equipment is required to service the aircraft since almost all systems are located at waist or chest height.

After several years of operations, it was found that it was necessary to rebuild the wings due to stress cracks in the fifteen percent wing spar. Many of the aircraft were subsequently rebuilt, with titanium keel members and a rewire and avionics update. The CF-5 fleet was approaching the end of its planned 4000 hour life expectancy by the early 1980s. To enable the continued use of the aircraft as fighter lead in trainers (FLIT) for the CF-18 Hornet fighter, a role for which it had been used since 1985, two major upgrades were undertaken. These would provide an Estimated Life Expectancy (ELE) until 2005 or later, and extend the airframe life to 6000 hours.

In early 1987 a contract was issued to Bristol Aerospace Ltd., located at Winnipeg International Airport, to rebuild fifty-eight aircraft (thirty-three CF-5A and twenty-three CF-5D), later revised to thirty-six (thirteen CF-5A and twenty-three CF-5D). Under this Depot Level Inspection and Repair Program (DLIR) the aircraft underwent twenty-nine in-depth inspections as recommended by Northrop Corporation. Under the Life Extension Program (SLEP), a complete detailed inspection was made of all structural components and repairs as required including reinforcement and replacement of the dorsal longeron by a stainless steel component, and replacement of five aft fuselage formers. The FS325 to FS362 bulkheads and intake duct skins were replaced (see station diagrams on pages 42 and 43). New, redesigned wings were installed and the vertical stabilizer was reskinned. Both main and nose landing gear were replaced, as were all fuel cells and flight control bearings. Finally, the aircraft were completely rewired.

In November 1990 a second program, titled the Avionics Update Program (AUP) was initiated in forty-four aircraft (eleven CF-5a and thirty-three CF-5D). Several of the avionics systems installed in the aircraft required replacement, since their maintenance could no longer be supported. As well, an avionics upgrade was required to allow the aircraft to meet its role as lead in trainer for the CF-18 Hornet fighter.

To meet these requirements several new systems were installed. A Heads-Up Display and Weapons Aiming Computer System (HUDWACS) and an Interface Electronics Unit replaced the no longer supportable gunsight. An Inertial Navigation System (INS) Ring Laser Gyro was installed enabling accurate navigational information to be transmitted to the HUDWACS to improve the accuracy of the information for weapons delivery. To improve debriefing of pilot training missions, a video camera and TEAC recorder were added. An Up Front Controller to provide central control of the HUDWACS, navigation and communication systems was installed, and the existing analog Air Data Computer was replaced by a Miniature Standard Air Data Computer to enable the transmission of digital information to the HUDWACS and Inertial Navigation System. The existing UHF radio was replaced by an ARC-164 unit with a HAVE QUICK capability. To improve the safety of flight, an APN-194(V) radar altimeter with a micro voice message system, and a standby altitude indicator system were installed. Finally, an angle of attack sensor and "G" measuring system was installed to provide more accurate sensor information. The first upgraded aircraft was rolled out in August 1989 and test flown on 14 June 1991.

In order to validate the life extension program for the CF-5 fleet, a full scale durability and damage tolerance test (FSDADTT) was undertaken. Aircraft 116729 received all the DLIR structural improvements before being seconded to Canadair Ltd. for testing in April, 1988. The aircraft was subjected to loading which simulated actual fighter pilot training using current flight profile information. No major unexpected failures were discovered in the test aircraft after the completion of 24,000 hours of testing in March 1995. It was concluded that the life of the CF-5 aircraft fleet could be safely extended to 6000 hrs. of flying the aircraft in the Fighter Lead In Training role.

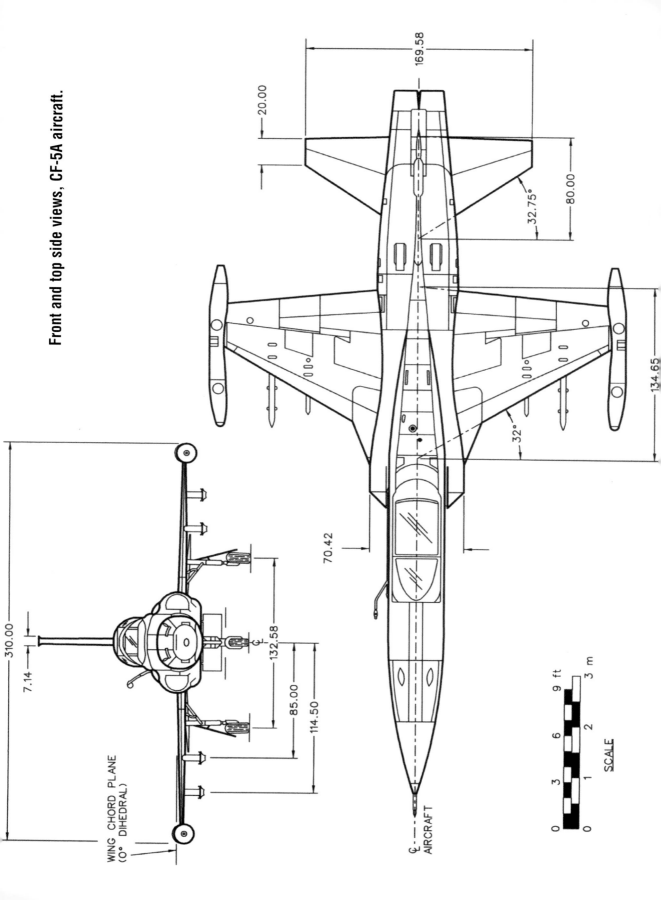

Front and top side views, CF-5A aircraft.

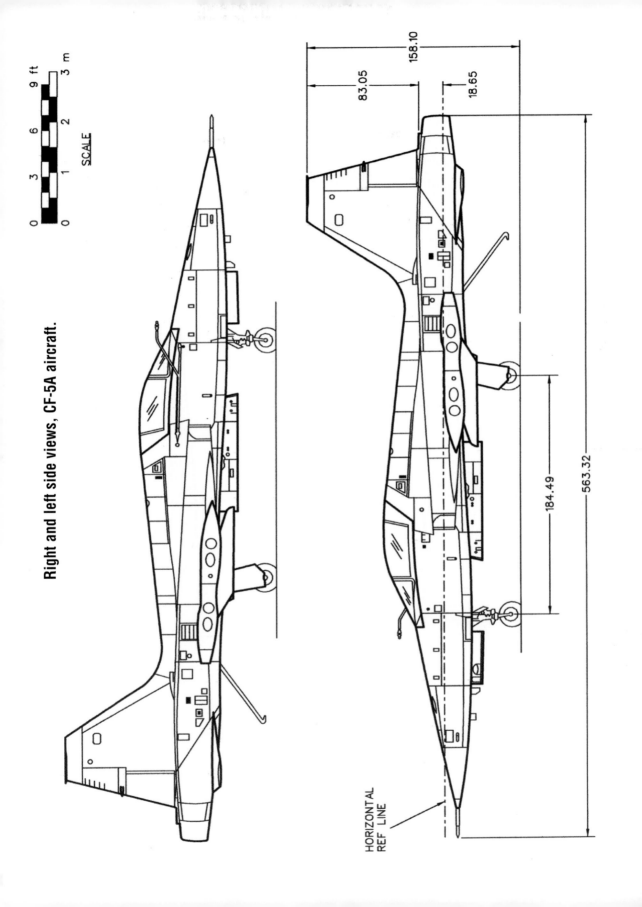

Right and left side views, CF-5A aircraft.

SCALE

0   3   6   9 ft

0   1   2   3 m

158.10

83.05

18.65

563.32

184.49

HORIZONTAL
REF LINE

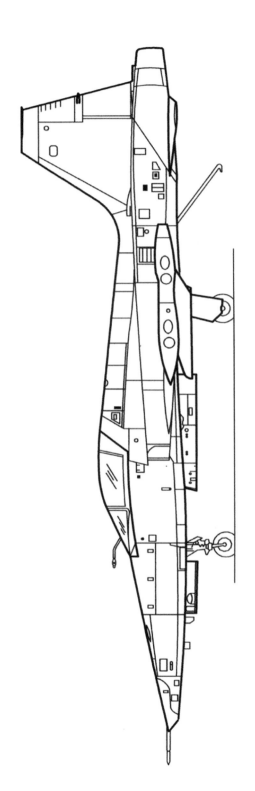

Right and left side views, CF-5AR aircraft.

SCALE

9 ft
3 m
6
2
3
1
0
0

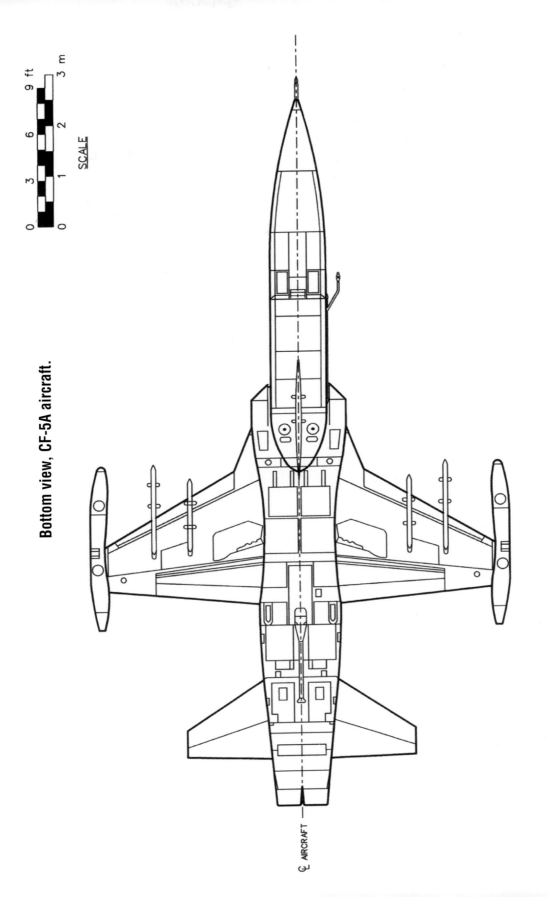

Bottom view, CF-5A aircraft.

SCALE

9 ft

3 m

℄ AIRCRAFT

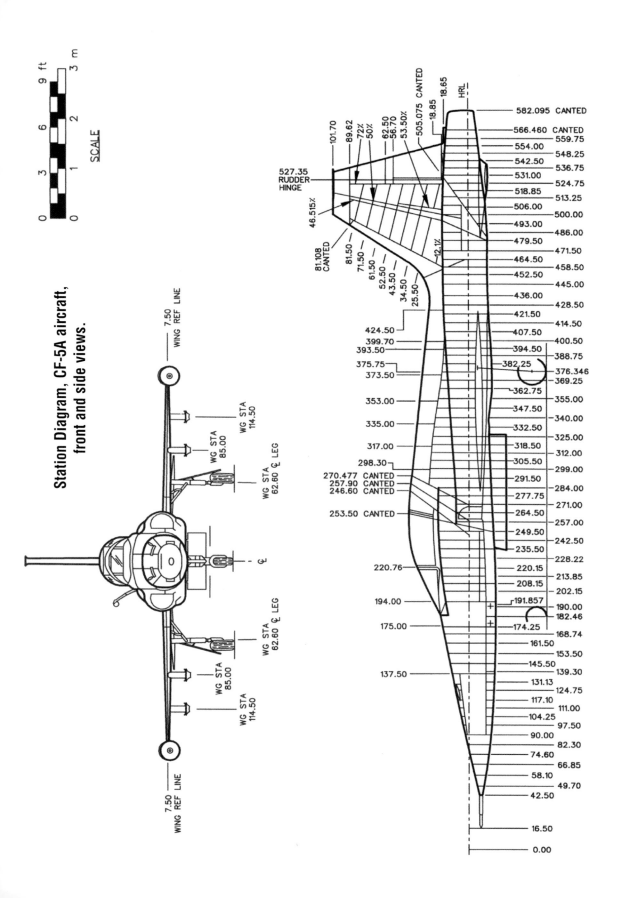

Station Diagram, CF-5A aircraft, front and side views.

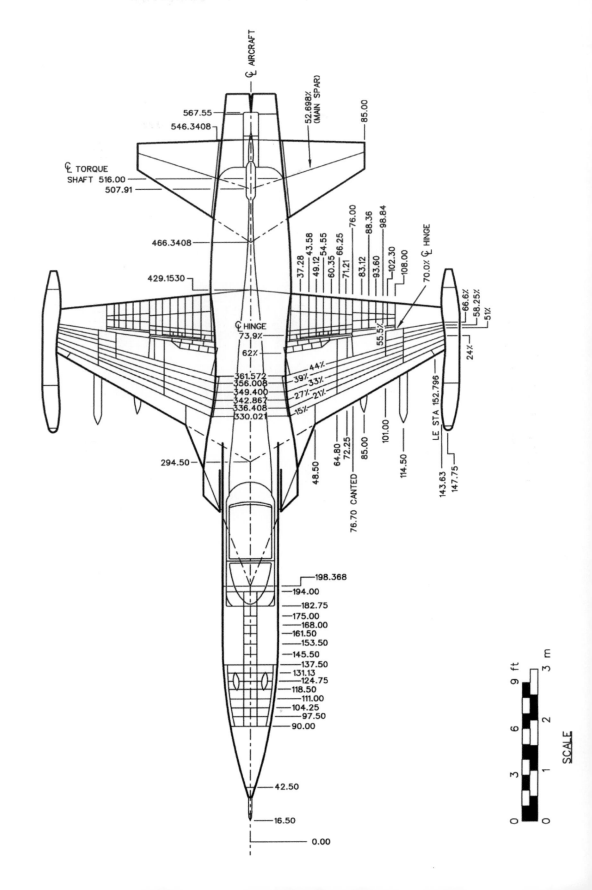

Station Diagram, CF-5A aircraft, top view.

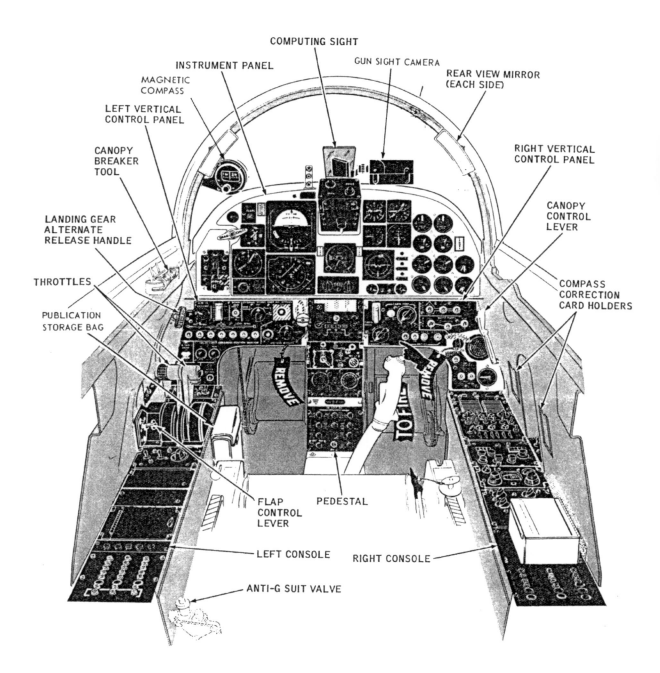

COMPUTING SIGHT

INSTRUMENT PANEL

GUN SIGHT CAMERA

REAR VIEW MIRROR
(EACH SIDE)

MAGNETIC
COMPASS

LEFT VERTICAL
CONTROL PANEL

RIGHT VERTICAL
CONTROL PANEL

CANOPY
BREAKER
TOOL

CANOPY
CONTROL
LEVER

LANDING GEAR
ALTERNATE
RELEASE HANDLE

THROTTLES

COMPASS
CORRECTION
CARD HOLDERS

PUBLICATION
STORAGE BAG

FLAP
CONTROL
LEVER

PEDESTAL

LEFT CONSOLE

RIGHT CONSOLE

ANTI-G SUIT VALVE

Cockpit layout, CF-5A.

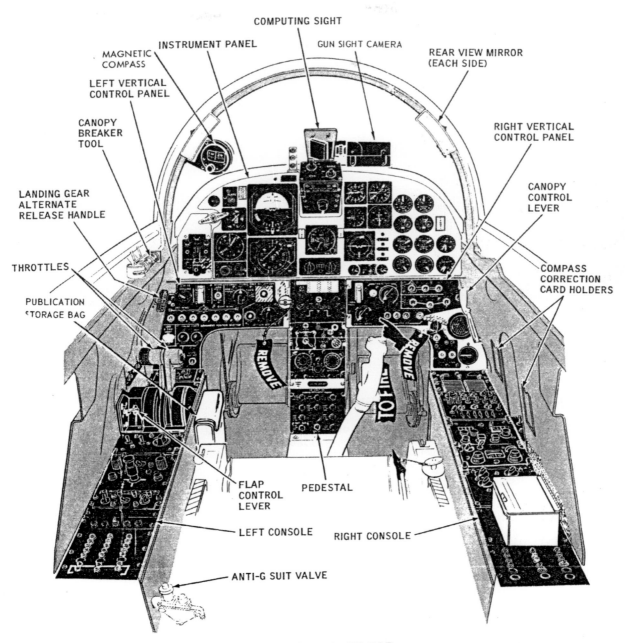

COMPUTING SIGHT

INSTRUMENT PANEL

GUN SIGHT CAMERA

MAGNETIC COMPASS

REAR VIEW MIRROR (EACH SIDE)

LEFT VERTICAL CONTROL PANEL

CANOPY BREAKER TOOL

RIGHT VERTICAL CONTROL PANEL

CANOPY CONTROL LEVER

LANDING GEAR ALTERNATE RELEASE HANDLE

THROTTLES

COMPASS CORRECTION CARD HOLDERS

PUBLICATION STORAGE BAG

FLAP CONTROL LEVER

PEDESTAL

LEFT CONSOLE

RIGHT CONSOLE

ANTI-G SUIT VALVE

Cockpit layout, CF-5AR.
Note CCS-1 (Camera Control System 1) module controls in left side console.

CF-5D serial no. 116843, in service with 1 CFFTS, Cold Lake, in flight over Northern Alberta. The distinctive shape of the aircraft is evident in this photo.

(DND, Neg. No.RE 75-1518)

CANADAIR CF-5D FREEDOM FIGHTER

Canadair designator CL-219-1A17, CTS Control Number CF116D

Description:	Two seat, all metal construction, advanced operational training fighter aircraft.
Powerplant:	Two General Electric J-85 CAN-15 (Orenda-built) turbojet engines 2820 lbs. (1281 kg.) thrust, 2925 lbs.(1329.5 kg.) thrust military power 4300 lb. (1950 kg) thrust, with afterburning
Dimensions:	Wingspan with tip tanks 25.10 ft (7.87m) Length 46.4 ft (14.13m) Height 13.1 ft (4.01m) Wing Area 174 ft2 (16.16m2)
Weights:	Empty 9384 lbs. (4265 kg.) Takeoff weight without external stores 14,150 lbs. (6418 kg.) Maximum takeoff weight 20,390 lbs. (9249 kg.)
Performance:	Max speed sea level at 11,630 lbs. (5276 kg.) in clean configuration, M 1.04 Max speed at 30,000 ft. (9144 m.) in clean configuration, M 1.36 Takeoff distance at 13,400 lbs. (6078 kg.) 1900 ft. (579 m) Max rate of climb 33,000 ft/min (10,058 m/min)
Armament:	A variety of combinations of externally mounted ordnance and/or externally mounted fuel tanks. The CF-5D carried no internally mounted cannon (see Chapter 6)

Front view of CF-5D 116843. Note greater fuselage depth compared to CF-5A.

(A. Stachiw)

Three-quarter front starboard side view of CF-5D 116843.

(A. Stachiw)

Starboard side view of CF-5D 116843.

(A. Stachiw)

Three-quarter starboard side rear view of CF-5D 116843.

(A. Stachiw)

Rear view of CF-5D 116843.

(A. Stachiw)

As in the case of the CF-5A, the structure of the CF-5D aircraft is broken down into small units for manufacture and ease of replacement in the event of damage. Spares for both single and two seat models are eighty percent interchangeable aft of the canted bulkhead behind the cockpit.

The forward fuselage contains the electronic equipment, nose gear, communications and navigation equipment, and the cockpits, ejection seats and controls. The upper longerons serve as the cockpit rails and support the canopies. A strengthened cockpit windscreen and canopy offered greater protection against bird strikes, anti-icing equipment was improved, and additional armour protection was provided. The windscreen is a one piece curved panel providing an unobstructed view forward, and is hinged at its forward end to provide easy access to the rear of the instrument panel. Each cockpit has a separate canopy, which is raised and lowered manually by a lever on the right inside wall of the cockpit, saving weight and maintenance time. External jettison controls are provided on both sides of the aircraft.

Cockpit canopies in open position of CF-5D 116842   *(A. Stachiw)*

View of rear fuselage of CF-5D 116846 showing area rule configuration. Note smooth finish and clean appearance of the aircraft in the aluminum finish scheme.   *(A. Stachiw)*

Nose landing gear of CF-5D 116842.

(A. Stachiw)

Main landing gear of CF-5D 116842

(A. Stachiw)

Front and top views, CF-5D aircraft

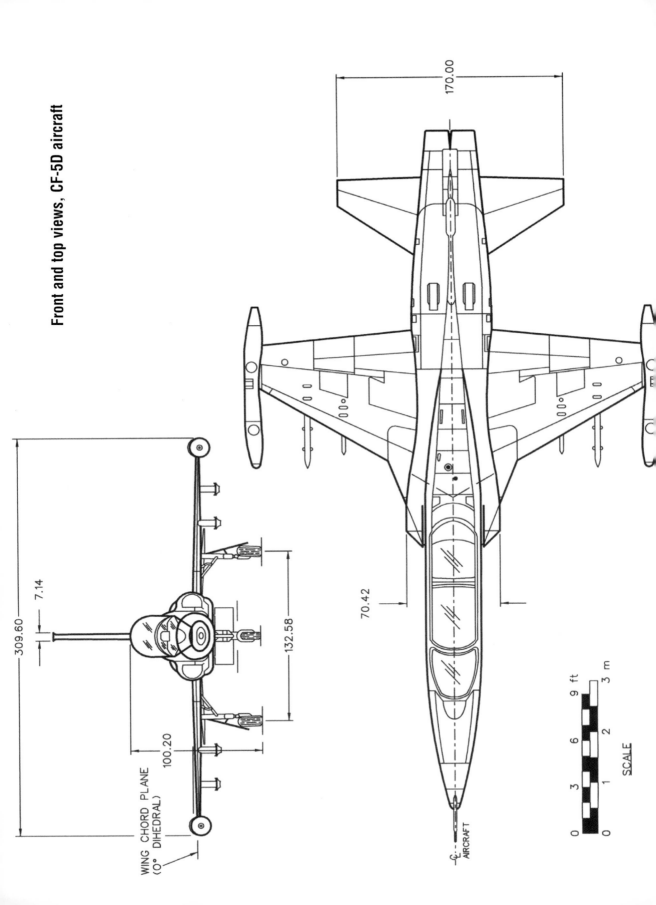

170.00

70.42

309.60

7.14

132.58

100.20

WING CHORD PLANE
(0° DIHEDRAL)

C. AIRCRAFT

9 ft

3 m

3   6   2

0   1

3   6

0   0

SCALE

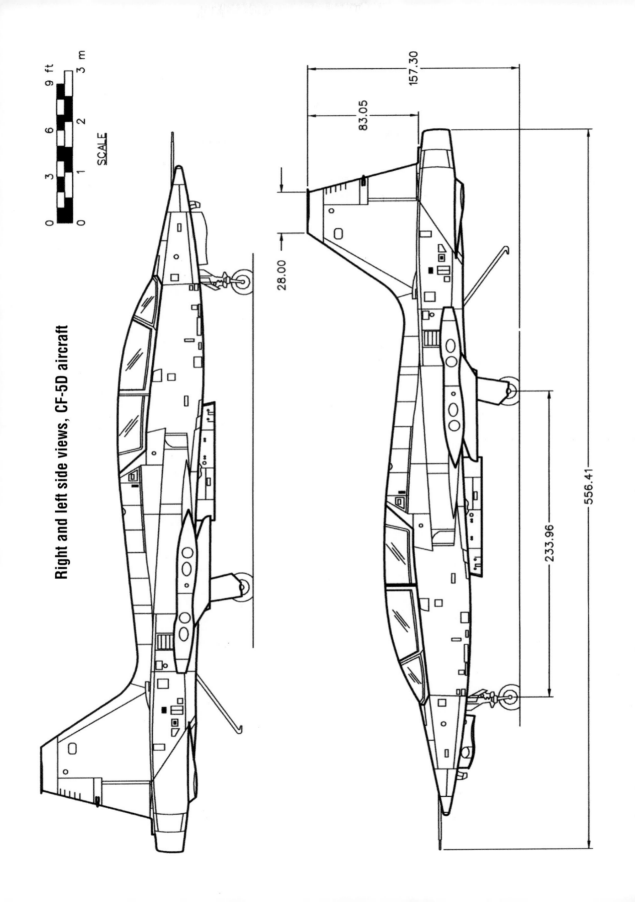

Right and left side views, CF-5D aircraft

Bottom view, CF-5D aircraft

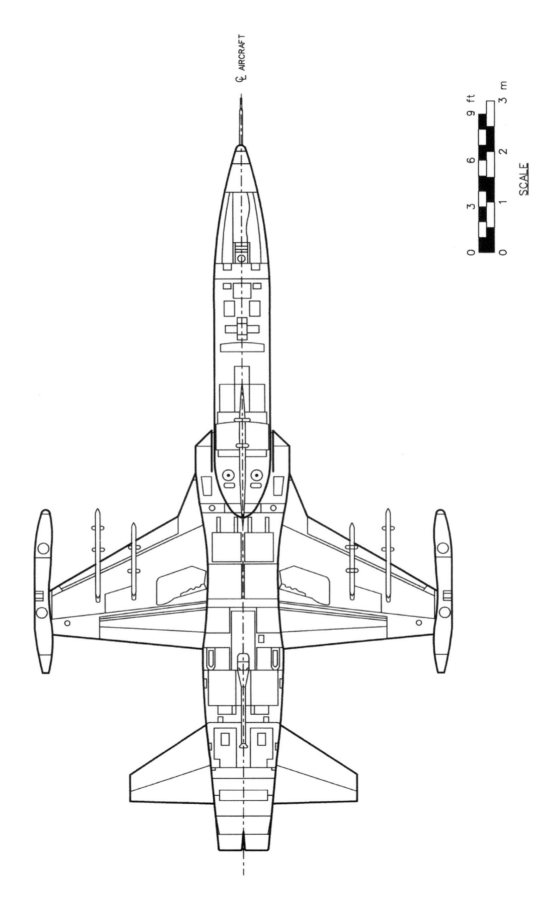

℄ AIRCRAFT

SCALE

0   3   6   9 ft
0   1   2   3 m

Station Diagram, CF-5D aircraft, front and side views

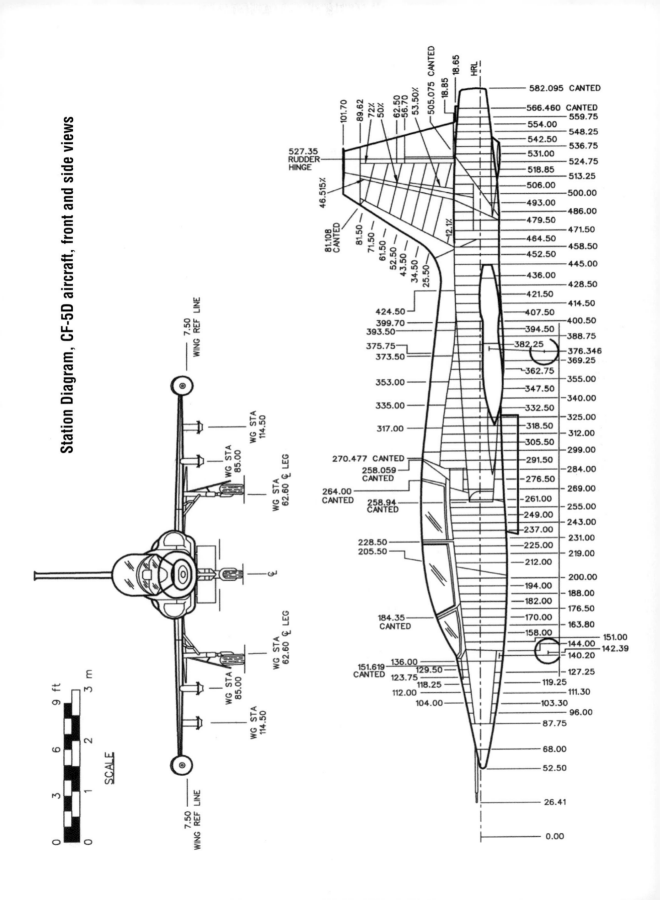

Station Diagram, CF-5D aircraft, top view.

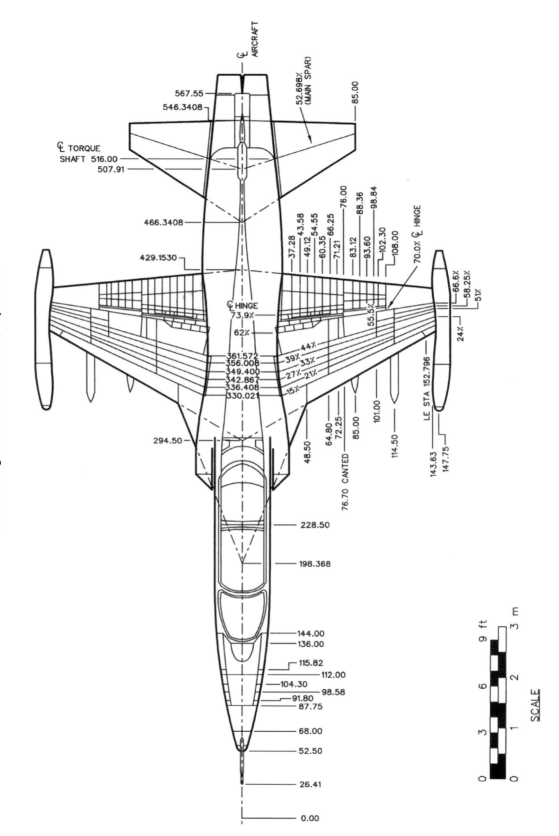

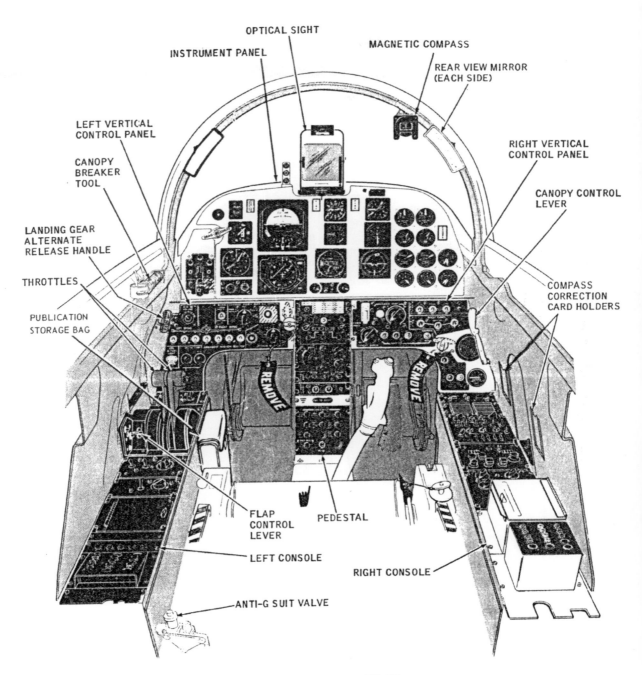

Front cockpit layout, CF-5D

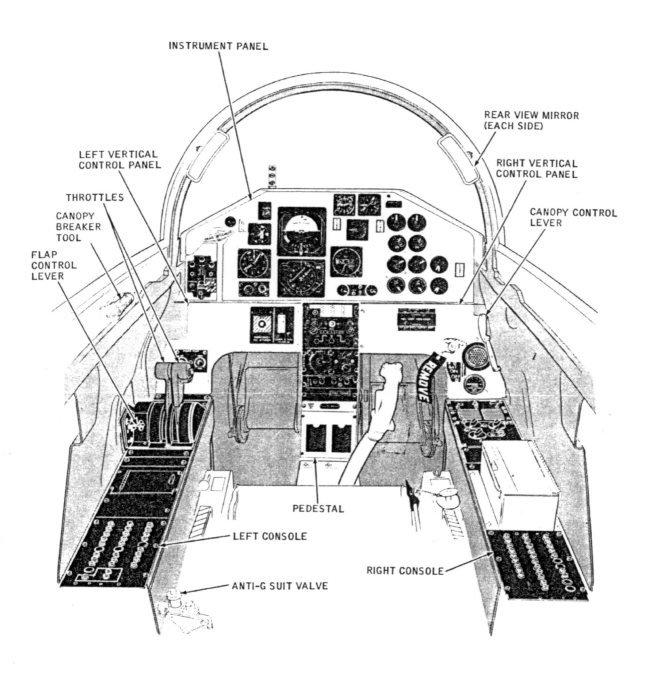

INSTRUMENT PANEL

REAR VIEW MIRROR
(EACH SIDE)

LEFT VERTICAL
CONTROL PANEL

RIGHT VERTICAL
CONTROL PANEL

THROTTLES

CANOPY CONTROL
LEVER

CANOPY
BREAKER
TOOL

FLAP
CONTROL
LEVER

PEDESTAL

LEFT CONSOLE

RIGHT CONSOLE

ANTI-G SUIT VALVE

Rear cockpit layout, CF-5D

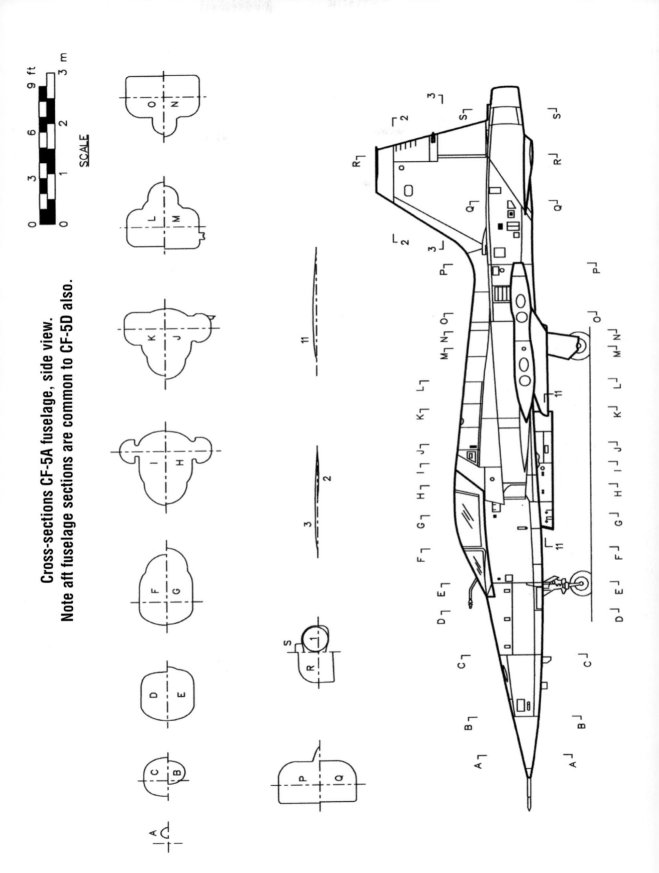

**Cross-sections CF-5A fuselage, side view.
Note aft fuselage sections are common to CF-5D also.**

SCALE

9 ft
6
3
0

3 m
2
1
0

Cross-sections particular to CF-5D fuselage, side view.

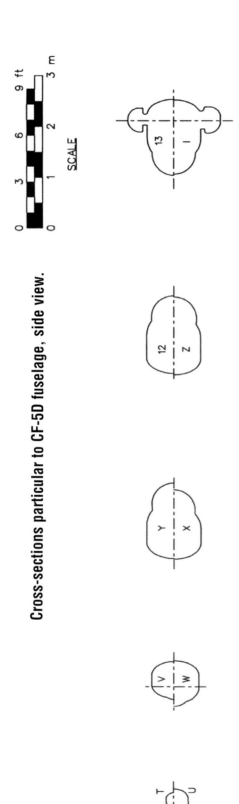

SCALE

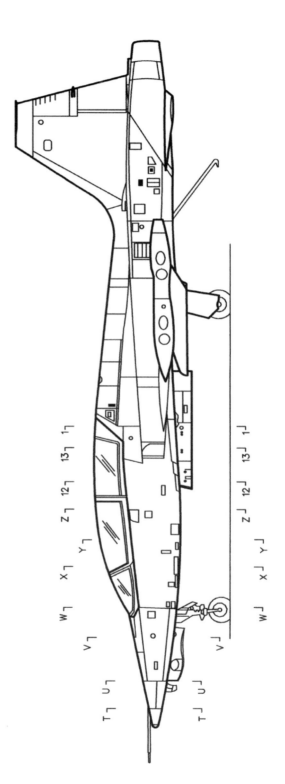

Cross-sections CF-5A top view.

CHAPTER FOUR

CF-5 Squadrons and Units

Northrop F-5B serial no. 63-8445 during testing by CEPE. This aircraft was subsequently used as the prototype for the YF-5B-21, testbed for the F-5F. *(Canadair Ltd., Neg. No. 49913)*

448 Test Squadron

Central Experimental and Proving Establishment (CEPE)

Aeronautical Engineering Test Establishment (AETE)

As the flying unit of the Aeronautical Engineering Test Establishment (AETE), 448 Test Squadron was tasked with the technical evaluation of new aircraft for service with Canada's Armed Forces, test flying of new aircraft to establish flight parameters and procedures, and test flying of modifications incorporated in aircraft. The unit was formed on 4 May 1967 at

Cold Lake, Alberta, and incorporated in the Canadian Armed Forces on 1 February 1968. The Central Experimental and Proving Establishment (CEPE), as the higher establishment was previously named, had been based at RCAF Station Uplands before relocating to CFB Cold Lake. The squadron was disbanded on 1 September 1971, and all aircraft and personnel were absorbed by the Aeronautical Engineering Test Establishment.

Stock Northrop F-5 aircraft, both single (e.g. serial no. 58-38421) and two seat (e.g. serial no. 58-38445) models, were test flown by pilots of CEPE prior to the delivery of the Canadair-built aircraft. These aircraft, still wearing their USAF serial numbers, had rudimentary Canadian markings applied for public relations purposes.

Northrop F-5A serial no. 63-8421 during testing at Central Experimental and Proving Establishment, Uplands. This aircraft subsequently served with the Turk Hava Kuvvetleri (Turkish Air Force).

(DND Photo Neg. No. PL-145520)

Both CF-5A and CF-5D aircraft were taken on strength with 448 Test Squadron at AETE. The first CF-5A, serial no. 14701, later 116701, had been taken on strength by AETE on 2 February 1968. It was flown in a Canadian Forces CC130 Hercules to Edwards AFB in California, where it was written off on 3 December 1969 while undergoing flight testing. It was struck off strength on 19 May 1970. The second CF-5A, serial no. 116702, was taken on strength on 5 June 1969 and remained in service at AETE throughout its service

life. The first CF-5D, serial no. 116801, was taken on strength 31 October 1968 and initially flew with the RQU Detachment of AETE at Edwards AFB, and thereafter at Cold Lake until its retirement. In 1996 it was part of a group of CF-5 aircraft sold to the Botswana Defence Force, having been dismantled and flown to Botswana by Antonov AN24 charter.

While in service with AETE at Cold Lake, aircraft wore the distinctive red "X" symbol on the vertical stabilizer. As well, 116702 wore a white flash on each side.

A CF-5A, serial no. 116721, in service with AETE, in original three-colour variegated camouflage colour scheme, wearing the distinctive red "X" on the vertical stabilizer.

(A. Stachiw)

408 "Goose" Transport Support and Area Reconnaissance Squadron

408 Tactical Strike and Area Reconnaissance Squadron

408 "Goose" Tactical Fighter Squadron

On 11 February 1964 an organization order was issued transferring 408 Squadron from RCAF Station Rockcliffe to Rivers, Manitoba. Designated 408 Transport Support and Area Reconnaissance Squadron (TS&AR Sqn), the unit, now equipped with T-33AN Silver Star Mk.3 and C-47 Dakota aircraft was joined on 1 May by the Transport Support Flight, equipped with C-119 Boxcar transports. Plans were already underway to replace the Dakota and Boxcar aircraft with the C-130B Hercules, and pilots were taking the conversion course to the Hercules run by 435 Squadron at Namao, Alberta.

By May 1964 the squadron was equipped with eight T-33s, four equipped with the photo reconnaissance nose installation, and four as tactical strike fighters with underwing pylons and .50 cal. machine guns in the nose, to provide firepower in support of ground troops. The C-119s were replaced by four C-130B Hercules aircraft by 11 June 1965, and the T-33 strength was increased to nine.

Armourer raises 500 lb. bomb into position on underwing pylon of T-33AN Silver Star aircraft 21118 of 408 Squadron. Note 408 Squadron "Goose" insignia on vertical stabilizer above flag.

(DND, Neg.No. CF66-614-2)

Armourer adjusts .50 cal. machine gun in nose of T-33AN Silver Star aircraft.

(DND, Neg.No. CF66-614-3)

T-33AN Silver Star aircraft 21633 in reconnaissance camera nose configuration overflies a burned out tank on range at Station Rivers, Manitoba.

(DND, Neg.No. CF66-615)

On 15 March 1966 CFB Rivers was taken over by Mobile Command. The squadron was transferred from Air Transport Command to Mobile Command, and redesignated as 408 Tactical Strike and Area Reconnaissance Squadron (TacS&AR Sqn). The Hercules flight remained within Air Transport Command as a detachment of 435(T) Squadron. The last C-47 Dakota was retired on 8 November 1966, and 408 Squadron was now equipped with only T-33AN aircraft. With the T-33s, the squadron continued training in the tactical strike and ground support role, including trials developing airborne chemical warfare spray operations against troop concentrations.

In early 1967, in anticipation of the new CF-5 aircraft coming on strength, the squadron was tasked to provide contact training for pilots selected to become instructors on CF-5s. One of the seven pilots selected was from 408 Sqn., the remainder from 434 Sqn, a recently disbanded CF104 unit. The number of T-33s was doubled to eighteen in April 1967 to accomplish the additional training requirement. In May, two Northrop test pilots visited Rivers with F-5 aircraft to give familiarization flights, and the squadron began looking forward to operating the new fighter. Pilot training in the reconnaissance and tactical support roles was intensified.

On 1 February 1968 the unification of the Canadian Armed Forces was made official. During that month, 434 Squadron was reactivated as the Operational Training Squadron for the introduction of the CF-5 aircraft. During that spring, the first seven pilots selected to become CF-5 instructors, including one from 408 Squadron, departed for Williams AFB in Nevada for training on the new fighter at 4441 Combat Crew Training Squadron. In September, the training program was changed to qualify pilots in either tactical support or photo reconnaissance, while maintaining the minimum operational standard in the alternate role. On 1 October 1968 the squadron was redesignated 408 Tactical Fighter Squadron (TAC(F) Sqn), and became part of 10 Tactical Air Group.

In 1969, 408 Squadron reached twenty-five years of service and became eligible to receive its Standard. Because of the length of time necessary to produce the Standard, the ceremony was scheduled for mid 1970. At the same time, planning was underway to convert the squadron to operate the CF-5 aircraft. However, the runways at CFB Rivers were too short to support CF-5 operations, and the relocation of the squadron to CFB Namao, as well as other bases, was considered. Before any definite plans for a move were decided, it was announced that the squadron, which had pioneered the tactical air support of the army in the postwar years, would be disbanded, never having operated the CF-5 aircraft.

The Standard presentation was made on 20 March 1970 in a ceremony at CFB Rivers. The squadron was officially disbanded on 1 April 1970, being reactivated on 1 January 1971 as 408 Tactical Helicopter Squadron.

1 Canadian Forces Flying Training Squadron

419 "Moose" Tactical Fighter (Training) Squadron

In December 1950 RCAF Station Gimli, Manitoba was reactivated to support the operations of No.2 Flying Training School, committed to training pilots for the RCAF and the NATO training program. In June 1953, 2 FTS was redesignated 3 Advanced Flying School (3 AFS) and in September began to operate the Canadair produced T-33AN Silver Star Mk.3 jet trainer, as well as the North American Harvard piston engine trainers. By August 1954, 3 AFS, redesignated No.1 FTS, became an all-jet-equipped school, using Canadair CT114 Tutors for the basic training course, and the T-33 for advanced training.

In 1970 the CT114 Tutors were moved to CFB Moose Jaw, to be operated there by 2 Canadian Forces Flying Training School (2 CFFTS), and the T-33s from Moose Jaw were moved to Gimli. On 1 September 1971 CFB Gimli was closed, and the move of 1 CFFTS to Cold Lake, which had begun in December 1970 was completed. The first course at Cold Lake graduated on 10 December 1971.

In September 1973 the Canadair CT133 Silver Star Mk.3 was officially retired as the advanced pilot trainer of the Canadian Forces, and was replaced by the Canadair CF116D Freedom Fighter. On 2 December 1973 the first of the graduates from the basic flying courses at 2 CFFTS based at Moose Jaw were received for advanced flying training at 1 Canadian Forces Flying Training School (1 CFFTS).

Personnel of 1 CFFTS pose in front of the new CF-5D advanced pilot trainer which replaced the CT133 Silver Star Mk.3 visible in the background. *(DND, Neg.No. CK74 285)*

Canadair CF-5 Freedom Fighter

The first graduate on the CF-5 course is congratulated. *(DND, Neg.No. CK 74 286)*

During 1974 personnel at 1 CFFTS were completely converted to the operation of the CF-5, and on 22 October 1974 the first class graduated on the new trainer.

On 2 May 1975 official approval was given to retitle 1 CFFTS as 419 Fighter Training Squadron. On 1 November 1975, 419 Tactical Fighter (Training) Squadron was reactivated, assuming the role of advanced flying training and operational training. The squadron, which had previously flown CF-100 Canuck fighters, had stood down as 419(AW) F Sqn on 31 December 1962.

Initially, the students received instruction in the Basic Fighter Pilots Course. The curriculum would be further expanded in the years to follow. The flying course consisted of first, the conversion phase, in which the student was taught to fly the CF-5. Included in this phase were clearhood, or visual flying, instrument flying, night and formation flying. This was followed by the tactical phase, in which the student learned the use of the aircraft as a weapons platform. Elements included were low level navigation, air-to-ground weapons delivery, air-to-ground attack, night formation flying, visual reconnaissance, advanced handling, high level tactical

formation flying, basic fighter manoeuvres, air-to-air DART, and air-to-air refueling.

In addition, a comprehensive ground school course included aircraft operation, aerodynamics, fighter tactics, tactical formation, low level navigation, air to ground weapons delivery, ground attack tactics, weapons, weapon effects and target requirements, enemy defences, penetration aids, laser and electro-optical bombs, rear hemisphere aerial attack systems, all aspect aerial attack systems, aerial attack tactics, enemy air-to-air systems and tactics, reconnaissance systems, NORAD and land forces indoctrination and equipment recognition training.

As well, the Fighter Weapons Instructors Course (FWIC) was conducted once a year. This ten week post graduate course was the epitome of fighter flying and instruction. The course included air-to-air combat, weapons and weapons effects, ground attack tactics, and advanced air-to-air firing, as well as academic subjects. The course was based on many hours of tactical flying in both CF-5 and CF104 aircraft, and the graduates became both exceptional pilots and instructors.

The first course commenced in January 1976. All future CF-5 pilots were to be trained at 419 Fighter Training Squadron, and pilots destined to fly the CF101B Voodoo and CF104 Starfighter were to be given their initiation into high performance flight in the CF-5, as was previously done by 434 TACF(T) Squadron. With the conversion of 433e ETAC to the CF-18 Hornet and disbandment of 434 Tactical Fighter Squadron, the role of the squadron changed to Lead In Fighter Training and adversary training for the CF-18 Hornet. All serviceable CF-5 aircraft were taken on strength of 419 Fighter Training Squadron.

Squadron personnel also participated annually in Dissimilar Air Combat Training, both in the United States at the Red Flag Exercises, and, at home in Cold Lake in the Maple Flag Exercise. These exercises provided the pilots with the opportunity to stay current in tactical roles, flying against adversaries from other NATO countries. In the early 1990s, with the arrival of the newly updated CF-5 aircraft, the squadron acquired an enhanced capability in their role of preparing pilots to fly the CF-18 Hornet fighters.

A CF-5A, serial no. 116703, "Bruce the Moose", presentation aircraft of 419F(T) Sqn. This was the first of three such decorated aircraft. *(A. Stachiw)*

A CF-5D, serial no. 116823, in service with 419F(T) Sqn. The aircraft is finished in the Ghost Aggressor scheme with the distinctive "last two" of its serial number in red characters on the forward fuselage.

(A. Stachiw)

On 25 June 1995 the squadron was disbanded at CFB Cold Lake, and the CF-5 aircraft was retired from operational duty. The squadron was reactivated on 23 July 2000 at CFB Cold Lake to conduct Phase IV of the NATO Flying Training Program, operating the CT155 Hawk aircraft for Lead In Fighter Training.

433 "Porcupine" Tactical Fighter Squadron

433e "Porc Epic" Escadrille Tactique de Combat

On 15 February 1961 an Organization Order had been issued disbanding 433AW(F) Sqn, then flying Avro Canada CF-100 Mk.5 all weather fighters at North Bay, Ontario in Air Defence Command. The unit number remained dormant until 22 November 1968, when Lieutenant Colonel C.A. LaFrance received the order to reform the squadron. Designated 433e Escadrille Tactique de Combat, a predominantly French language unit, the squadron was to be based at Bagotville, Quebec, where it reformed on 26 September 1969 in Mobile Command. Equipped with the Canadair CF-5 Freedom Fighter, the first of which was flown in to the base on 18 November 1969 by Lt Frank Senechal, the squadron was built up to a strength of fourteen aircraft by the end of 1970. This included both CF-5A single seat fighters and CF-5D dual seat operational trainers. As well, the squadron was set up as a completely self supporting unit capable of field operations in support of the army keeping with the operational mandate of Mobile Command.

Two sections were formed, one specializing in ground attack, the other in tactical reconnaissance, although aircrew were required to be proficient in both roles. A period of intense training in ground attack, interdiction, armed reconnaissance and aerial combat occupied the unit's activities over the following period of time. A change in national defence policies resulted in the assigning of further responsibilities for the squadron. In support of the Canadian government's claim to the Arctic regions, the squadron undertook patrol of these, and reconnaissance of the territorial waters off the northern and eastern coasts.

A trio of CF-5 aircraft in service with 433e ETAC. Note the squadron "Porc-Epic" emblem on the fuselage just aft of the engine intake. The nearest aircraft, serial no. 116748, is fitted with the reconnaissance nose.

(A. Stachiw)

A CF-5D, serial no. 118813 in service with 433e ETAC. The squadron emblem is featured on the nose of the aircraft. *(Greg Marshall)*

In 1972, two 433e ETAC aircraft were deployed to Europe to participate in Operation Fencer, to evaluate the use of the CF-5 in support of the defence of the Northern Flank of Europe by NATO. As well, that year in Exercise Plein Vol four CF-5s were deployed to the base at Nancy-Ochey, France in support of the Franco-Canadian cooperation program. The base was the home of Escadrille 1/3 Navarre, of the Armee de l'Air, the sister squadron of the "Porc-Epics". This exercise was followed by several further deployments to France, Norway, Denmark and Germany over the next three years.

When Canada sold twenty CF-5 aircraft to Venezuela in 1972, pilots from 433e ETAC and 434 TacF(OT) squadrons were used to ferry the aircraft by way of Puerto Rico. The delivery flights took place between February and May of that year after the aircraft had been refinished in Venezuelan colours by Field Aviation at CFB Trenton. Captain Hank Morris and two other pilots and twelve ground crew had spent the previous six months in Venezuela training the Venezuelan personnel in the flying and maintenance of the aircraft.

When the role in support of the defence of the Northern Flank of Europe by NATO was assigned to the Canadian Forces, the CF-5s were flown across the Atlantic to Norway, refueled enroute by the Canadian Forces Boeing CC137 tanker aircraft of 437 "Husky" Transport Squadron based at Trenton. In preparation for this tasking, squadron aircrew underwent intensive training in air-to-air refueling techniques. The first trans-Atlantic deployment took place on 9 June 1973, when four aircraft from 433e ETAC along with four from 434 TACF(OT) Squadron were flown non-stop to Andoya, Norway in exercise Long Leap I. Several weeks of operations there proved the feasibility of the operations. Over a year later, in exercise Long Leap II, the squadron deployed to Denmark to train with the Royal Danish Air Force.

With the creation of Air Command, 433e ETAC remained in 10 Tactical Air Group, but was transferred from Mobile Command to Air Command. Although the new base maintenance policy was implemented at that time, 433e ETAC continued to assume the responsibility of maintaining its own aircraft. Exercises for operational readiness continued as before, with the squadron participating in the Open Challenge competitions. Deployments to various locations in Canada and the United States were continued to maintain the mobility necessary in the squadron's tactical support role as was participation in competitions. The squadron took part in exercises at the US Marine Corp Air Combat Maneuvering Range at Yuma, Arizona, and the Red Flag exercises at Nellis AFB in Nevada, where competitions simulating wartime operations against Warsaw Pact forces were held.

Emphasis on offensive air support as a primary role in 433e ETAC's commitment to the defence of the Northern Flank of Europe gained prominence in the 1980s. In March 1980 the system of tactical evaluations (Tac Evals) was introduced, giving opportunity for the units to test operational capabilities and to establish priorities in the tactical support role. On 15 July 1982 Fighter Group was created, ending the last direct link between 433e ETAC and 10 Tactical Air Group and Mobile Command, the role of the squadron becoming operational tactical fighter.

The squadron received its colours on 6 July 1985, marking twenty-five years of operations. On 19 April 1986 a ceremony was held at Bagotville marking the end of CF-5 Freedom Fighter operations, and the squadron's seventeen year association with the aircraft. The squadron now operates the CF-18 Hornet fighter from its base at 3 Wing, CFB Bagotville.

434 "Bluenose" Tactical Fighter (Operational Training) Squadron

434 "Bluenose" Tactical Fighter Squadron

On 1 March 1967, 434 Strike Attack Squadron was disbanded at Zweibrucken, Federal Republic of Germany. The squadron had operated CF104 Starfighter aircraft, and F-86 Sabre fighters before that, in 3 Wing, 1 Canadian Air Division in NATO. The squadron was reactivated as 434 Tactical Fighter (Operational Training) Squadron [434TACF(OT) Sqn] on 15 February 1968 at Canadian Forces Base Cold Lake, operating under Mobile Command. The Commanding Officer was LCol O.B. Philp, who had commanded 434 Squadron as a CF104 unit. Among the varied roles assigned to the unit were close air support, interdiction, photo and visual reconnaissance, air superiority, and the training for those roles. All future CF-5 pilots were to be trained at 434 Squadron, and pilots destined to fly the CF104 Starfighter were to be given their initiation into high performance flight in the CF-5.

CF-5A, serial no. 116712 of 434 "Bluenose" TACF(OT) Sqn with the distinctive schooner emblem on the tailband, and the barely visible 434 "Speedbird" insignia on the fuselage side just aft of the engine intake.

(Robert Bryden)

CF-5D, serial no. 116822 in service with 434 TACF(OT) Sqn. The 434 "Speedbird" insignia on the fuselage side aft of the engine intake is more in evidence on the well-worn finish scheme. Note the underwing tank on the inboard wing pylon, and the LAU-5003 rocket pod on the outer wing pylon.

(Robert Bryden)

During the spring and summer of 1968, ten pilots selected to become CF-5 instructors, including one from 408 Squadron, departed for Williams AFB in Nevada for training on the new fighter, at 4441 Combat Crew Training Squadron. Each were given thirty hours of transition, air combat, air gunnery, ground attack and night flying. Additional personnel were taken on strength during that summer as the squadron prepared for the arrival of the new fighter.

Although the squadron was initially equipped with the T-33AN Silver Star Mk.3, the first CF-5 aircraft were taken on strength in January 1969 and an average of three were received in each of the following months. The first course, beginning in April, was a pre-CF104 course. This was followed in May by the first CF-5 course, in which the initial cadre of pilots who were to form 433e ETAC, based at Bagotville, began their training. As well, the first four pilots from the Royal Netherlands Air Force underwent training on the CF-5, followed by five others. They were to form the nucleus of 313 Squadron RNAF, which, equipped with NF-5B aircraft, was formed in the Netherlands early in 1970 to be the Operational Conversion Unit. These pilots were to ferry the first four NF-5s to the Netherlands in November 1969 in Operation Hi-Flite.

In 1970, under Operation Fence Phase 1, the value of the CF-5 to the defence of the Northern Flank of Europe was analyzed. The squadron was deployed to the Canadian base at Baden, Federal Republic of Germany, by way of Goose Bay, Greenland, Iceland, and Prestwick in Scotland.

Back in Canada, on 2 May 1970 squadron pilots set two cross-Canada speed records. Captains J. Miller and R. Small each flew from Victoria, British Columbia to Shearwater, Nova Scotia, with Capt. Miller setting a record of 4 hours, 24 minutes and 53 seconds, covering 2800 miles at an average speed of 636 mph. On 1 July 1970 Captain P. Pattison set a record in the opposite direction, flying from Shearwater to Victoria in 5 hours, 34 minutes and 21 seconds, flying into the prevailing winds. The flight was to commemorate the 50th anniversary of the first cross-Canada mail flight in 1920, which was accomplished in ten and a half days. As well, in October, 434 Squadron participated in the first CF-5 Tactical Air Meet, titled Open Challenge I, which was to be held annually to compete for excellency in tactical operations.

In February 1971 the squadron deployed to Whitehorse, Yukon Territory, participating in Exercise Northern Pioneer, gaining experience operating in Arctic conditions, which was to be repeated many more times in the future. Another speed record was set when Capt. J. Swallow flew the 1220 mile distance from Inuvik, North West Territories, to Edmonton in 2 hours and 40 seconds. As well, during 1971, the CF-5 training course was increased to ninety hours. The new syllabus now included training in reconnaissance, air combat, tactics, and air-to-air weaponry.

In January 1972 as part of the sale of surplus CF-5 aircraft to Venezuela, the squadron began training three Venezuelan pilots and twenty-nine technicians at Cold Lake. In addition, thirteen officers and men were sent to Venezuela for six months to train the VAF in operating and maintaining a CF-5 Operational Training Unit (see Chapter 2). Also during January, the squadron deployed to Fort St. John, British Columbia for six days. As part of Exercise On Top III, the squadron's ability to conduct operations from a forward base was evaluated. In February the squadron participated in Exercise Rapier Thrust III out of CFB Comox, British Columbia, and in May deployment to CFB Shilo, Manitoba, to participate in exercises which involved providing close air support. In addition to the squadron's functions in providing operational training, participation in competitions, exercises and deployments were to become the mainstay of the squadron's activities over the next few years.

On 1 December 1975, 434 Tactical Fighter Operational Training Squadron [434TACF(OT) Sqn] was relieved of its training role, and was redesignated 434 Tactical Fighter Squadron [434 TAC(F) Sqn]. On 1 November 1975, 419 Tactical Fighter (Training) Squadron had been reactivated, assuming the role of advanced flying training and operational training. The role of 434 Squadron changed to Rapid Reaction Squadron, standing ready to deploy to Norway on NATO's Northern Flank in the event of hostilities.

In March 1980 the system of tactical evaluations (Tac Evals) was introduced, giving opportunity for the units to test operational capabilities and to establish priorities in the tactical support role. On 15 July 1982 Fighter Group was created, ending the last direct link between 434 TAC(F) Sqn and 10 Tactical Air Group and Mobile Command, the role of the squadron becoming operational tactical fighter.

On 15 July 1982 the squadron moved to CFB Bagotville, sharing the base with 433e ETAC. The squadron was moved again in 1985 to CFB Chatham, New Brunswick and in 1986 became the only operational CF-5 squadron, when 433e ETAC began operating CF-18 Hornet fighters from CFB Bagotville. The squadron disbanded in June 1988 at CFB Chatham, and all CF-5s were assigned to 419 Fighter (Training) Squadron at CFB Cold Lake, operating in the training role. The "Bluenose" Squadron was reactivated on 5 July 1992 at CFB Shearwater as 434 (Composite) Squadron, flying Canadair CE-144 Challenger and Canadair CE133 Silver Star Mk.3 aircraft in the Electronic Counter Measures training role, and on fleet support duties.

CHAPTER FIVE

CF-5 Colour Schemes and Markings

A trio of CF-5D Freedom Fighter aircraft of 419 TAC(F) Squadron in Aggressor finish schemes flying near CFB Cold Lake.

(DND, Neg.No. IOC82-048)

Over the approximately twenty-seven years that the CF-5 Freedom Fighter fleet was in service with the Canadian Forces, the finish and markings applied to the aircraft underwent several changes which reflected the different roles in which the aircraft was employed. The original three-colour variegated camouflage scheme applied to the CF-5A was suitable for the tactical support role that the fighter was originally intended to fulfill. In time, with the application of the fleet to the role of lead in trainer for the front line CF-18 Hornet, the colour scheme was changed to reflect current practice in aircraft colour schemes, and to represent Aggressor aircraft.

In the case of the CF-5D, the original high visibility aluminum colour scheme with red search markings was suitable to the training role of the two seat aircraft. In time, most of the aircraft were refinished in a variety of Aggressor style schemes to represent the aircraft in service with Soviet and other Warsaw Pact Air Forces. These various schemes, originally developed by the US Air Force and the US Navy for their Red Flag and Top Gun programs, were adopted by the Canadian Forces. Initial drawings were prepared, based on the USAF Technical Orders, documenting the patterns, colours, lettering and national markings featured on the aircraft. The identifying numbers of these drawings are noted following the descriptions of these various schemes.

Mr. Patrick Martin has prepared the definitive work on this subject titled *Canadian Armed Forces, Aircraft Finish & Markings, 1968-1997*. The book covers the finish schemes and markings applied to all Canadian Forces aircraft and should be consulted for the exhaustive treatment of this subject, with not only text and photographs, but representations of the official Canadian Forces drawings as well. One section is devoted to the CF-5 Freedom Fighter aircraft, covering all the schemes that are described in this section.

The marking features presented in the following illustration are referred to in the text describing the various colour schemes in this chapter. The markings are as follows:

1. Red Shadow lettering CANADIAN ARMED FORCES / FORCES ARMÉES CANADIENNES
   Black lettering CANADIAN ARMED FORCES / FORCES ARMÉES CANADIENNES
2. ROUNDEL IDENT and ROUNDEL
3. CAF
4. FLAG - LOW VIZ and FLAG - BORDERED
5. Red Shadow Lettering CANADA and Black/Grey Lettering CANADA
6. Canada Wordmark
7. Canadian Forces Signature

CANADIAN ARMED FORCES
FORCES ARMÉES CANADIENNES

1.

CANADIAN ARMED FORCES   FORCES ARMÉES CANADIENNES

2.      3. CAF   4.

6.   7.

5. CANADA
   CANADA
      Canadian Forces   Forces Canadiennes

Common markings featured on Canadian Forces CF-5 aircraft.

CF-5A 116768 in three-colour variegated camouflage colour scheme with bilingual markings.
Note the "Canadian Armed Forces" marking on the port side aft fuselage.

(DND, Neg.No. PCN71-427)

CF-5A 116785 in three-colour variegated camouflage colour scheme with bilingual markings, 15 October 1971.
Note the "Forces Armées Canadiennes" marking on the starboard side aft fuselage, and the Last Three Numbers
of the Aircraft Serial Number in white above the flag.

(Douglas Remington, via Patrick Martin Collection)

5.1: CF-5A Three-Colour Variegated Camouflage Colour Scheme

This colour scheme was featured on the CF-5A aircraft as the factory delivery finish.

5.1.1: CF-5A Three-Colour Variegated Camouflage Colour Scheme with Bilingual English / French Markings

This finish scheme was documented on the Canadian Forces Drawings 51868, "Finish Scheme, Camouflage (Variegated) CF-5A ACFT" and 51869, "Identification Markings, Camouflage, CF-5A ACFT," Cancelled, 7 February, 1973.

The three-colour variegated camouflage colour scheme featured upper surface colours CGSB Green 503-301 (close to FS.595 34084) and Grey 501-302 (close to FS.595 36118), with the whole underside finished in Grey 101-327.

The national markings were bilingual, with English (Canadian Armed Forces) on the port side of the aft fuselage and French (Forces Armées Canadiennes) on the starboard side, in 4-inch letters, with a full colour 12-inch diameter roundel on both sides of the aircraft just aft of the engine air intake. On each side of the vertical stabilizer, there was a full colour 12-inch Canadian Flag, later outlined in a white or aluminum border, with the full Aircraft Serial Number under the flag in 4-inch numbers. At the units, the Last Three Numbers of the Aircraft Serial Number were applied later in 12-inch white numbers above the flag for easier identification of the aircraft. These numbers were either broken stencil style or full numbers, and were not included on any official drawing. There were no upper or underwing markings. A black outline of the walk area was applied to the upper wings, but later removed. All lettering and numbers were in CGSB Black 501-301.

5.1.2: CF-5A Three-Colour Variegated Camouflage Colour Scheme with Symmetrical Markings

This finish scheme was documented on the Canadian Forces Drawing C72F00330, "Finish Scheme and Identification Markings, Camouflage (Variegated) CF116 (CF-5A) ACFT".

This variation of the three-colour variegated camouflage colour scheme featured upper surface colours CGSB Green 503-301 (close to FS.595 34084) and Grey 501-302 (close to FS.595 36118), with the whole underside finished in Grey 101-327.

CF-5A 116758 in three-colour variegated camouflage colour scheme with symmetrical markings in service with 434 TACF(OT) Squadron. Note the "Bluenose" insignia on the vertical stabilizer.

(Richard J. De Launais)

CF-5A 116785 in two-colour wraparound variegated camouflage colour scheme with toned down markings in service with 434 TAC(F) Squadron.

(Richard J. De Launais)

The national markings featured a 12-inch Roundel Ident in full colour, on the forward fuselage ahead of the windscreen. The bilingual markings, which had been declared illegal by the International Civil Aviation Authority (ICAO) were replaced by the word CANADA in 4-inch black in the same position, on both sides of the fuselage. On each side of the vertical stabilizer, there was a full colour 12-inch Canadian Flag, outlined in a white border, with the full Aircraft Serial Number under the flag in 4-inch numbers. At the units, the Last Three Numbers of the Aircraft Serial Number were applied later in 12-inch white numbers above the flag for easier identification of the aircraft. These numbers were either broken stencil style or full numbers. There were no upper or underwing markings. All lettering and numbers were in CGSB Black 501-301.

Unit markings were applied to both sides of the upper vertical stabilizer and aft of the engine air intake, port side only. 433e ETAC featured the "Porc Epic" (Porcupine) emblem in a disc just aft of the engine air intake, port side only, while 434 TACF(OT) Squadron featured a "434 Speedbird" emblem just aft of the engine air intake, port side only, and the "Schooner" emblem on both sides of the upper vertical stabilizer.

5.2: CF-5A Two-Colour Wraparound Variegated Camouflage Colour Scheme

This colour scheme was a variation of the factory delivery finish.

5.2.1: CF-5A Two-Colour Wraparound Variegated Camouflage Colour Scheme with Symmetrical Markings

This finish scheme was documented on the Canadian Forces Drawing 8240502, "Finish Scheme and Identification Markings, Camouflage (Variegated) CF116 (CF-5A) ACFT".

The two-colour wraparound variegated colour scheme featured the colours CGSB Green 503-301 (close to FS.595 34084) and Grey 501-302 (close to FS.595 36118) wrapped around both upper and lower surfaces.

The national markings featured a 12-inch Roundel Ident in full colour, on the forward fuselage ahead of the windscreen. On each side of the vertical stabilizer, there was a full colour 12-inch Canadian Flag outlined in a white border, with the full Aircraft Serial Number under the flag in 4-inch numbers. Both the Roundel Ident and Canadian Flag were later toned down by removing the white. The CANADA in 4-inch letters was retained in the same position, each side of the aft fuselage. On the upper surface of both wings, a full colour 16-inch roundel was applied, later toned down by the removal of the white. Under the starboard wing, in 12-inch letters, CAF was applied, and under the port wing, in 12-inch numbers, the Last Three Numbers of the Aircraft Serial Number, both facing forward. The Last Three Numbers of the Aircraft Serial Number were applied on the interior and exterior surfaces of the nosewheel door (not in evidence in photos). All lettering and numbers were in CGSB Black 501- 301.

A later variation featured the same markings, but all in Black 501-301

5.2.2: CF-5A Two-Colour Wraparound Variegated Camouflage Colour Scheme with Federal Identity Program Markings

This finish scheme was documented on the Canadian Forces Drawing 8240502, "Finish Scheme and Identification Markings, Camouflage (Variegated) CF116 (CF-5A) ACFT".

This variation of the two-colour wraparound variegated camouflage colour scheme featured the colours CGSB Green 503-301 (close to FS.595 34084) and Grey 501-302 (close to FS.595 36118) wrapped around both upper and lower surfaces.

The Federal Identity Program national markings featured a 12-inch roundel on the fuselage just aft of the engine air intake, and the 140mm Canada Wordmark on the aft fuselage, with a 100mm Canadian Forces Signature on the forward fuselage ahead of the windscreen, on both sides. There was a 12-inch Canadian Flag, with the full Aircraft Serial Number under the flag in 4-inch numbers on both sides of the vertical stabilizer. A false canopy was applied to the lower fuselage. All markings were in CGSB Black 501-301. There is no evidence of this scheme having been applied to any aircraft.

CF-5A 116705 in the early Ghost Aggressor variegated colour scheme with symmetrical markings in service with 419 F(T) Squadron.

(DND, Neg.No.CXC 85-2017)

5.3: CF-5A Ghost Aggressor Variegated Colour Scheme

The Ghost variegated scheme was based on USAF T.O. 23-1-23A camouflage finish for the F-5E Aggressor aircraft, with FS595 colours Grey 36251, Grey 36307and Blue 35237 upper surfaces and Blue 35622 underside surfaces.

5.3.1 CF-5A Ghost Aggressor Variegated Colour Scheme with Symmetrical Markings

This finish scheme was documented on the Canadian Forces Drawing 8740339, "Finish Scheme and Identification Markings, Ghost Scheme, CF116 (CF-5A) AC".

The CAF adaptation of the Ghost Aggressor variegated colour scheme featured the same FS.595 colours Grey 36251, Grey 36307, and Blue 35237 in a wraparound pattern encompassing both upper and lower surfaces.

The national markings featured a 12-inch Roundel Ident, red and blue only, with lettering in CGSB Black 512- 301, on both sides of the fuselage just aft of the intake, 4-inch CANADA, on both sides of the fuselage in Black 512-301, the 12-inch Canadian Flag, in red only, on each side of the vertical stabilizer, with the full Aircraft Serial Number

under the flag in 6-inch Black 512-301 numbers. There were no markings on the upper surfaces of the wings. The letters CAF were applied in 12-inch letters under the starboard wing facing forward, with the Last Three Numbers of the Aircraft Serial Number in 12-inch numbers under the port wing, also facing forward, both in CGSB Black 512-301. The Last Two Numbers of the aircraft serial number were applied in 18-inch Aggressor style red numbers, outlined in yellow, below the windscreen, on both sides of the aircraft nose. A false cockpit was painted on the undersurface of the nose in CGSB Black 512-301.

5.3.2: CF-5A Ghost Aggressor Variegated Colour Scheme with Federal Identity Program Markings

This finish scheme was documented on the Canadian Forces Drawing 8740339, "Finish Scheme and Identification Markings, Ghost Scheme, CF116 (CF-5A) AC".

This variation of the Ghost Aggressor Variegated Colour Scheme featured the same FS.595 colours Grey 36251, Grey 36307, and Blue 35237 in a wraparound pattern encompassing both upper and lower surfaces.

The national markings featured a 12-inch roundel just aft of the intake opening, a 140mm Canada Wordmark on the

CF-5A 116765 in the Ghost Aggressor variegated colour scheme with Federal Identity Program markings in service with 419 F(T) Squadron.

(A. Stachiw)

aft fuselage, and a 100mm Canadian Forces Signature on the nose forward of the windscreen on both sides. The 20-inch Canadian Flag, with the full Aircraft Serial Number under the flag in 6-inch numbers and the unit marking above was on each side of the vertical stabilizer. A 16-inch roundel was applied, facing forward, on both the upper surface of the port wing and on the lower surface of the starboard wing. The Last Three Numbers of the Aircraft Serial Number were applied in 10-inch numbers, facing forward, on both the upper surface of the starboard wing and on the lower surface of the port wing. All markings in CGSB Grey 501-323. A false cockpit was painted on the undersurface of the nose, and, the Last Two Numbers of the Aircraft Serial Number were applied on the interior and exterior surfaces of the nosewheel door, both in CGSB Grey 501-302 (not in evidence in photos).

5.4: CF-5D Standard Aluminum Colour Scheme

This colour scheme was applied to all CF-5D aircraft as the factory delivery finish.

5.4.1: CF-5D Standard Aluminum Colour Scheme with Bilingual English / French Markings

This finish scheme was documented on the Canadian Forces Drawings 51866, "Finish Scheme, CF-5D ACFT" and 51867, "Identification Markings, CF-5D ACFT". Cancelled, 7 February 1973.

The standard aluminum colour scheme featured an overall finish of CGSB Aluminum 515-101, with CGSB Red 509-102 search markings on the upper and lower surfaces of the outer wings and tip tanks, and the horizontal stabilizers. The anti glare panel on the nose ahead of the windscreen and the engine intake area were finished in CGSB Black 512-301.

The national markings were bilingual, with English (Canadian Armed Forces) on the port side and French (Forces Armées Canadiennes) on the starboard side of the aft fuselage, both in 6-inch Red Shadow lettering. There was a full colour 16-inch roundel on each side of the nose ahead of the cockpit, with the 9-inch letters CAF to the left of the roundel and 9-inch Last Three Numbers of the Aircraft Serial Number to the right of the roundel. On each side of the vertical stabilizer, there was a full colour 29-inch Canadian Flag, initially with no aluminum border, with the full Aircraft Serial Number under the flag in 4-inch numbers. On the upper surface of both wings, facing forward, was a full colour 36-inch roundel. On the lower surface of the starboard wing, CAF was applied in 12-inch letters, and on the lower surface of the port wing, the Last Three Numbers of the Aircraft Serial Number were applied in 12-inch numbers, both facing forward. All lettering and numbers were in CGSB Black 501-301.

CF-5D 116826 in the standard aluminum colour scheme with bilingual markings in service with 434 TAC(F) Operational Training Squadron. *(John Lumley)*

CF-5D 116839 in the standard aluminum colour scheme with symmetrical markings in service with 1 CFFTS. Note the "Cold Lake" insignia on the tail band.

(Richard J. De Launais)

5.4.2: CF-5D Standard Aluminum Colour Scheme with Symmetrical Markings

This finish scheme was documented on the Canadian Forces Drawings C72F00329, "Finish Scheme and Identification Markings, CF-5D, CF116 ACFT". Cancelled, replaced by 8240504, "Finish Scheme and Identification Markings, CF116D (CF-5 DUAL) AC".

This variation of the Standard Aluminum Colour Scheme featured the same overall finish of CGSB Aluminum 515-101, with CGSB Red 509-102 search markings on the upper and lower surfaces of the outer wings and tip tanks, and the horizontal stabilizers. The anti glare panel on the nose ahead of the windscreen and the engine intake area were finished in CGSB Black 512-301.

The national markings featured a 12-inch Roundel Ident in full colour, on the forward fuselage under the windscreen, and the Last Three Numbers of the Aircraft Serial Number in 6-inch numbers on both sides of the fuselage just aft of the engine air intake. The bilingual markings, which had been declared illegal by the International Civil Aviation Authority (ICAO) were replaced by CANADA in 6-inch Red Shadow lettering in the same position, on both sides of the aft fuselage. On each side of the vertical stabilizer, there was a full colour 29-inch Canadian Flag, outlined with a white or aluminum border, with the full Aircraft Serial Number under the flag in 4-inch numbers, and unit markings above the flag.

On the upper surface of both wings, facing forward, was a full colour 36-inch roundel. On the lower surface of the starboard wing, CAF was applied in 12-inch letters, and on the lower surface of the port wing the Last Three Numbers of the Aircraft Serial Number were applied in 12-inch numbers, both facing forward. All lettering and numbers were in CGSB Black 501-301.

5.4.3: CF-5D Standard Aluminum Colour Scheme with Federal Identity Program Markings

This finish scheme was documented on the Canadian Forces Drawing 8240504, "Finish Scheme and Identification Markings, CF116D (CF-5 DUAL) AC".

This variation of the standard aluminum colour scheme featured the same overall finish of CGSB Aluminum 515- 101, with CGSB Red 509-102 search markings on the upper and lower surfaces of the outer wings and tip tanks, and the horizontal stabilizers. The anti glare panel on the nose ahead of the windscreen and the engine intake area were finished in CGSB Black 512-301.

The Federal Identity Program markings featured a full colour 16-inch roundel on both sides of the fuselage under the windscreen. A 140mm Canada Wordmark was placed just aft of the engine air intake, both sides, with a 100mm Canadian Forces Signature on the aft fuselage, both sides. On each side of the vertical stabilizer, there was a full colour

29-inch Canadian Flag, outlined with an aluminum border, with the Aircraft Serial Number under the flag in 4-inch numbers, and unit markings above the flag. A full colour 16-inch roundel was applied to both the top surface of the port wing and lower surface of the starboard wing, and the Last Three Numbers of the Aircraft Serial Number on the top surface of the starboard wing and on the lower surface of the port wing, all facing forward in 12-inch numerals. All lettering and numbers were in CGSB Black 501-301. This scheme was applied to a very few aluminum finished aircraft near the retirement of the fleet.

5.5: CF-5D Two-Colour Wraparound Variegated Camouflage Colour Scheme

This colour scheme was a variation of the factory delivery finish applied to the CF-5A aircraft.

5.5.1 CF-5D Two-Colour Wraparound Variegated Camouflage Colour Scheme with Original Markings

This finish scheme was documented on the Canadian Forces Drawing 8340053, "Finish Scheme and Identification Markings, Camouflage (Variegated), Standard Scheme CF116 (CF-5D) ACFT".

The two-colour wraparound variegated camouflage colour scheme featured the colours CGSB Green 503-301 (close to FS.595 34084) and Grey 501-302 (close to FS.595 36118), wrapped around both upper and lower surfaces.

The national markings featured a full colour 12-inch roundel just aft of the engine intake, and CANADA in 4-inch letters on the aft fuselage, on both sides. On each side of the vertical stabilizer there was a 12-inch Canadian Flag, which was toned down by removing the white, with the full Aircraft Serial Number under the flag in 4-inch numbers. The Last Two Numbers of the serial number in Aggressor style yellow numbers, outlined in red, was displayed on both sides of the nose, under the windscreen. On the upper surface of both wings, a 16-inch roundel was applied, later toned down by the removal of the white. Under the starboard wing, facing forward, CAF was applied in 12-inch letters, with 12-inch Last Three Numbers of the Aircraft Serial Number under the port wing, also facing forward. All lettering and numbers were in CGSB BLACK 501-301.

5.5.2: CF-5D Two-Colour Wraparound Variegated Camouflage Colour Scheme with Symmetrical Markings

This finish scheme was documented on the Canadian Forces Drawing 8340053, "Finish Scheme and Identification Markings, Camouflage (Variegated), Standard Scheme CF116 (CF-5D) ACFT".

CF-5D 116814 in two-colour wraparound variegated camouflage colour scheme with full colour markings in service with 419 F(T) Squadron.

(Patrick Martin)

This variation of the two-colour wraparound variegated camouflage colour scheme featured the same CGSB Green 503-301 (close to FS.595 34084) and Grey 501-302 (close to FS.595 36118) wrapped around both upper and lower surfaces.

The national markings featured a 12-inch Roundel Ident under the windscreen, and CANADA, in 4-inch letters on the aft fuselage, on both sides. On each side of the vertical stabilizer, there was a 12-inch Canadian Flag, with the full Aircraft Serial Number under the flag in 4-inch numbers. On the upper surface of both wings, a 16-inch roundel was applied. There were no underwing markings. The Last Two Numbers of the Aircraft Serial Number were applied on the interior and exterior surfaces of the nosewheel door. All markings were in CGSB Black 501- 301.

5.5.3: CF-5D Two-Colour Wraparound Variegated Camouflage Colour Scheme with Federal Identity Program Markings

This finish scheme was documented on the Canadian Forces Drawing 8340053, "Finish Scheme and Identification Markings, Camouflage (Variegated), Standard Scheme CF116 (CF-5D) ACFT".

This variation of the two-colour wraparound variegated camouflage colour scheme featured the same CGSB Green 503-301 (close to FS.595 34084) and Grey 501-302 (close to FS.595 36118) wrapped around both upper and lower surfaces.

The Federal Identity Program national markings featured a 12-inch roundel just aft of the engine air intake, a 140mm Canada Wordmark, on the aft fuselage, and a 100mm Canadian Forces Signature on the forward fuselage ahead of the windscreen, on both sides. On each side of the vertical stabilizer there was a 12-inch Canadian Flag, with the full Aircraft Serial Number under the flag in 4-inch numbers. A false cockpit was painted on the undersurface of the nose. All markings were in CGSB Black 501-301. There is no evidence of this scheme having been applied to any aircraft.

5.6: CF-5D Grape Aggressor Variegated Colour Scheme

The Grape variegated scheme was based on USAF T.O. 23-1-29 camouflage finish for the F-5E Aggressor aircraft, with FS.595 colours Blue 35414, Blue 35109 and Blue 35164 upper surfaces and Blue 35622 lower surfaces.

5.6.1: CF-5D Grape Aggressor Variegated Colour Scheme with Original Markings

This finish scheme was documented on the Canadian Forces Drawing 8340054, "Finish Scheme and Identification Markings, Grape Scheme CF116D (CF-5 DUAL) AC".

The CAF adaptation of the Grape Aggressor Variegated Colour Scheme featured the Tempo colours Blue 4700- BB-54

CF-5D 116807 in the Grape Aggressor variegated colour scheme with original markings at the Air Maintenance Development Unit, CFB Trenton.

(DND, Neg.No.TNC 77-5120)

(FS.595 35414), Blue 4700-BB-57 (FS.595 35109), and Blue 4700-BB-58 (FS.595 35164), with the whole underside finished in Blue 4700-BB-26 (FS.595 Blue 35622)

The national markings featured a full colour 12-inch roundel on the fuselage just aft of the engine air intake, 4-inch CANADA on the aft fuselage, and the Last Two Numbers of the serial number in 18-inch Aggressor style red numbers, outlined in yellow, under the windscreen, both sides. A full colour 20-inch Canadian Flag was applied to both sides of the vertical stabilizer, and the full Aircraft Serial Number was displayed under the flag in 4-inch numbers. There were no markings on the upper or lower surfaces of the wings. All lettering and numbers were in CGSB Black 512-301.

5.6.2: CF-5D Grape Aggressor Variegated Colour Scheme with Original Markings

This finish scheme was documented on the Canadian Forces Drawing 8340054, "Finish Scheme and Identification Markings, Grape Scheme CF116D (CF-5 DUAL) AC".

This variation of the Grape Aggressor wraparound variegated colour scheme featured the same FS.595 colours Blue 35414, Blue 35109 and Blue 35164 in a wraparound pattern encompassing both upper and lower surfaces.

The national markings featured a full colour 12-inch roundel just aft of the engine air intake, 4-inch CANADA aft of the wing, and the Last Two Numbers of the Aircraft Serial Number in 18-inch Aggressor style red numbers, outlined in yellow, under the windscreen on both sides. A full colour 20-inch Canadian Flag was applied to both sides of the vertical stabilizer, and the full Aircraft Serial Number was displayed under the flag in 4-inch numbers. There were no markings on the upper or lower surfaces of the wings. All lettering and numbers were in CGSB Black 512-301. A false cockpit was painted on the undersurface of the nose in CGSB Black 512-301.

5.6.3: CF-5D Grape Aggressor Wraparound Variegated Colour Scheme with Symmetrical Markings

This finish scheme was documented on the Canadian Forces Drawing 8340054, "Finish Scheme and Identification Markings, Grape Scheme CF116D (CF-5 DUAL) AC".

This variation of the Grape Aggressor wraparound variegated colour scheme featured the same FS.595 colours Blue 35414, Blue 35109 and Blue 35164 in a wraparound pattern encompassing both upper and lower surfaces.

The national markings featured a full colour Roundel Ident just aft of the engine air intake, 4-inch CANADA on the aft fuselage, and the Last Two Numbers of the Aircraft Serial Number in 18-inch Aggressor style red numbers, outlined in yellow, under the windscreen on both sides. A full colour 20-inch Canadian Flag was applied to both sides of the vertical stabilizer, and the full Aircraft Serial Number was displayed under the flag in 4-inch numbers. There were 16-inch roundels on the upper surfaces of both wings, and no underwing markings. All markings were in CGSB Black 512-301. A false cockpit was painted on the undersurface of the nose in CGSB Black 512-301. There is no evidence of this variation being applied to any aircraft.

5.6.4: CF-5D Grape Aggressor Wraparound Variegated Colour Scheme with Federal Identity Program Markings

This finish scheme was documented on the Canadian Forces Drawing 8340054, "Finish Scheme and Identification Markings, Grape Scheme CF116D (CF-5 DUAL) AC".

This variation of the Grape Aggressor wraparound variegated colour scheme featured the same FS.595 colours Blue 35414, Blue 35109 and Blue 35164 in a wraparound pattern encompassing both upper and lower surfaces.

The national markings featured a roundel on the side of the fuselage just aft of the air intake, the Canada Wordmark on the aft fuselage, and with the Canadian Forces Signature on the aircraft nose forward of the windscreen, both sides. A roundel was placed on the upper surface of the port wing and the undersurface of the starboard wing, and the Last Three Numbers of the Aircraft Serial Number were placed on the upper surface of the starboard wing and the under surface of the port wing. A false cockpit was painted on the undersurface of the nose. All markings were in CGSB Black 512-301. There is no evidence of this variation being applied to any aircraft.

5.7: CF-5D Faux Pas Aggressor Variegated Colour Scheme

The Faux Pas variegated scheme was not based on any known USAF specification.

5.7.1: CF-5D Faux Pas Aggressor Variegated Colour Scheme

This finish scheme was not documented on a Canadian Forces Drawing.

CF-5D 116815 in the Faux Pas Aggressor variegated colour scheme with original markings at the Air Maintenance Development Unit, CFB Trenton.

(DND, Neg. No. TNC 78-089)

The Faux Pas Aggressor variegated colour scheme featured FS.595 colours Blue 35488, Blue 35630 and Grey 36293 in a wraparound pattern encompassing both upper and lower surfaces.

The national markings featured a full colour 12-inch roundel on the side of the fuselage just aft of the air intake, 4-inch CANADA on the aft fuselage, and the Last Two Numbers of the Aircraft Serial Number in 18-inch Aggressor style red numbers with yellow outline under the forward cockpit on both sides. A full colour 20-inch Canadian Flag, with the full Aircraft Serial Number displayed under the flag in 4-inch numbers was displayed on both sides of the vertical stabilizer. There were no markings on the upper or lower surfaces of the wings. All lettering and numbers were in CGSB Black 512-301. A false cockpit was painted on the undersurface of the nose, and the Last Two Numbers of the Aircraft Serial Number were applied on the interior and exterior surfaces of the nosewheel door (not in evidence in photos), in CGSB Black 512-301.

5.7.2: CF-5D Faux Pas Aggressor Wraparound Variegated Colour Scheme with Symmetrical Markings

This finish scheme was not documented on a Canadian Forces Drawing.

This variation of the Faux Pas Aggressor variegated colour scheme featured FS.595 colours Blue 35488, Blue 35630 and Grey 36293 in a wraparound pattern encompassing both upper and lower surfaces.

This variation featured national markings with a 12-inch Roundel Ident, red and blue only, just aft of the air intake, 4-inch Canada on the aft fuselage, and the Last Two Numbers of the Aircraft Serial Number in 18-inch Aggressor style red numbers with yellow outline under the forward cockpit on both sides. A 20-inch Canadian Flag, red only, with the full Aircraft Serial Number under the flag in 4-inch numbers was displayed on both sides of the vertical stabilizer. There were no markings on the upper or lower surfaces of the wings. All lettering and numbers were in

CGSB Black 512-301. A false cockpit was painted on the undersurface of the nose, and the Last Two Numbers of the Aircraft Serial Number were applied on the interior and exterior surfaces of the nosewheel door in CGSB Black 512-301.

5.8: CF-5D Lizard Aggressor Variegated Colour Scheme

The Lizard variegated scheme was based on USAF T.O. 23-1-27A camouflage finish for the F-5E Aggressor aircraft, with FS.595 colours Green 35248, Brown 30118 and Yellow 33531 upper surfaces and Yellow 33531 lower surfaces.

5.8.1: CF-5D Lizard Aggressor Variegated Colour Scheme with Original Markings

This finish scheme was documented on the Canadian Forces Drawing 8340055, "Finish Scheme and Identification Markings, Lizard Scheme CF116D (CF-5 DUAL) AC".

The CAF adaptation of the Lizard Aggressor variegated colour scheme featured the same FS.595 colours Green 35248, Brown 30118 and Yellow 33531 upper surfaces and Yellow 33531 lower surfaces.

The national markings featured a 12-inch roundel in full colour, just aft of the engine air intake, 4-inch CANADA, on

the aft fuselage, and the Last Two Numbers of the Aircraft Serial Number in 18-inch Aggressor style red numbers with yellow outline under the forward cockpit on both sides. A 12-inch Canadian Flag in full colour was displayed on each side of the vertical stabilizer, with the full Aircraft Serial Number under the flag in 4-inch numbers. There were no upper or underwing markings. All lettering and numbers were in CGSB Black 512-301.

5.8.2: CF-5D Lizard Aggressor Variegated Colour Scheme with Symmetrical Markings

This finish scheme was documented on the Canadian Forces Drawing 8340055, "Finish Scheme and Identification Markings, Lizard Scheme CF116D (CF-5 DUAL) AC".

The CAF adaptation of the Lizard Aggressor variegated colour scheme featured the same FS.595 colours Green 35248, Brown 30118 and Yellow 33531 upper surfaces and Yellow 33531 lower surfaces.

The national markings featured a 12-inch Roundel Ident in full colour, just aft of the engine air intake, 4-inch CANADA on the aft fuselage, and the Last Two Numbers of the Aircraft Serial Number in 18-inch Aggressor style red numbers with yellow outline under the forward cockpit, on both sides. A 20-inch Canadian Flag in full colour was displayed on each side of the vertical stabilizer, with the full

CF-5D 116805 in the Lizard Aggressor variegated colour scheme with original markings at the Air Maintenance Development Unit, CFB Trenton.

(DND, Neg.No. TNC 77-5122)

Aircraft Serial Number under the flag in 4-inch numbers, There were no upper wing markings. Underwing, 12-inch CAF was applied under the starboard wing facing forward, with 12-inch Last Three Numbers of the Aircraft Serial Number under the port wing, also facing forward. All lettering and numbers were in CGSB Black 512-301. A false cockpit was painted on the undersurface of the nose in CGSB Black 512-301

5.8.3: CF-5D Lizard Aggressor Wraparound Variegated Colour Scheme

This finish scheme was documented on the Canadian Forces Drawing 8340055, "Finish Scheme and Identification Markings, Lizard Scheme CF116D (CF-5 DUAL) AC".

This variation of the Lizard Aggressor variegated colour scheme featured the same FS.595 colours Green 35248, Brown 30118 and Yellow 33531 in a wraparound pattern encompassing both upper and lower surfaces.

The national markings featured the Roundel Ident in full colour, just aft of the engine air intake, CANADA, on the aft fuselage, and the Last Two Numbers of the Aircraft Serial Number in 18-inch Aggressor style red numbers with yellow outline on the aircraft nose under the forward cockpit on both sides. A 12-inch Canadian Flag in full colour was displayed on each side of the vertical stabilizer, with the full Aircraft Serial Number under the flag. There were no upper wing markings. Underwing, the letters CAF were applied under the starboard wing facing forward, with the Last

CF-5D 116805 in the Lizard Aggressor variegated colour scheme with symmetrical markings. *(Richard J. De Launais)*

CF-5D 116809 in the Lizard Aggressor wraparound variegated colour scheme with original markings in service with 419 F(T) Squadron. *(Daniel Soulaine, via Patrick Martin)*

Three Numbers of the Aircraft Serial Number under the port wing, also facing forward. All lettering and numbers were in CGSB Black 512-301. A false cockpit was painted on the undersurface of the nose in CGSB Black 512-301

5.8.4: CF-5D Lizard Aggressor Wraparound Variegated Colour Scheme with Federal Identity Program Markings

This finish scheme was documented on the Canadian Forces Drawing 8340055, "Finish Scheme and Identification Markings, Lizard Scheme CF116D (CF-5 DUAL) AC".

This variation of the Lizard Aggressor variegated colour scheme featured the same FS.595 colours Green 35248, Brown 30118 and Yellow 33531 in a wraparound pattern encompassing both upper and lower surfaces.

The national markings featured a 12-inch roundel on each side of the fuselage just aft of the engine air intake, 140mm Canada Wordmark on each side of the aft fuselage, and with a 100mm Canadian Forces Signature on each side of the aircraft nose forward of the windscreen. A 20-inch Canadian Flag was displayed on each side of the vertical stabilizer, with the full Aircraft Serial Number under the flag in 4-inch numbers. A 16-inch roundel was placed on the upper surface of the port wing and the lower surface of the

starboard wing. The Last Three Numbers of the Aircraft Serial Number were placed on the upper surface of the starboard wing and on the lower surface of the port wing in 10-inch numerals. A false cockpit was painted on the undersurface of the nose in CGSB Black 512-301. The Last Two Numbers of the Aircraft Serial Number were applied on the interior and exterior surfaces of the nosewheel door. All markings were in F.S.595 Yellow 33434. There is no evidence of this variation being applied to any aircraft.

5.9: CF-5D Ghost Aggressor Variegated Colour Scheme

The Ghost variegated scheme, was based on USAF T.O. 23-1-23A camouflage finish for the F-5E aggressor aircraft, with FS.595 colours Grey 36251, Grey 36307 and Blue 35237 upper surfaces and Blue 35622 underside surfaces.

5.9.1: CF-5D Original Ghost Aggressor Variegated Colour Scheme

This finish scheme was documented on the Canadian Forces Drawing 8040262, "Finish Scheme and Identification Markings, Ghost Scheme CF116D (CF-5 DUAL) AC".

CF116D 116823 in the original Ghost Aggressor variegated colour scheme at the Air Maintenance Development Unit (AMDU), CFB Trenton. *(DND, Neg.No. TNC 77-5872)*

CF116D 116811 in the Ghost Aggressor variegated colour scheme with symmetrical markings.

(A. Stachiw)

The CAF adaptation of the Ghost Aggressor variegated camouflage scheme featured Tempo Grey 4700-B54 (FS595 36251), Tempo Grey 4700-B42 (FS 595 36307), and Tempo Blue 4700-BB69 (FS 595 35237) colours in a wraparound pattern encompassing both upper and lower surfaces.

The national markings featured a 12-inch roundel, in full colour, just aft of the intake, CANADA, in 4-inch letters on the aft fuselage, and the Last Two Numbers of the Aircraft Serial Number in 18-inch Aggressor style red numbers, outlined in yellow, under the windscreen on both sides. A 12-inch Canadian Flag in full colour was displayed on each side of the vertical stabilizer, with the full Aircraft Serial Number under the flag in 4-inch numbers. There were no upper or underwing markings. All lettering and numbers were in CGSB Grey 501-302.

5.9.2: CF-5D Ghost Aggressor Variegated Colour Scheme with Symmetrical Markings

This finish scheme was documented on the Canadian Forces Drawing 8040262, "Finish Scheme and Identification Markings, Ghost Scheme CF116D (CF-5 DUAL) AC".

This variation of the Ghost Aggressor variegated camouflage scheme featured the same FS.595 colours Grey 36251, Grey 36307, and Blue 35237 in a wraparound pattern encompassing both upper and lower surfaces.

The national markings featured a 12-inch Roundel Ident, red and blue only, just aft of the engine intake, CANADA in 4-inch letters on both sides of the aft fuselage in CGSB Grey 501-302, and the Last Two Numbers of the serial number in 18-inch Aggressor style red numbers, outlined in yellow, under the windscreen on both sides. A 12-inch Canadian Flag, in red only, was displayed on each side of the vertical stabilizer, with the full Aircraft Serial Number under the flag in 4-inch numbers. A 16-inch roundel, red and blue only, was applied to both upper wing surfaces. Under the starboard wing facing forward, CAF was applied in 12-inch letters, with the Last Three Numbers of the Aircraft Serial Number under the port wing in 12-inch numbers, also facing forward. All lettering and numbers were in CGSB Grey 501-302. A false cockpit was painted on the undersurface of the nose in CGSB Black 512-301.

CF-5D 116839 in the Ghost Aggressor variegated colour scheme with interim Federal Identity Program markings.
(Richard J. De Launais)

5.9.3: CF-5D Ghost Aggressor Variegated Colour Scheme with Interim Federal Identity Program Markings

This finish scheme was documented on the Canadian Forces Drawing 8040262, "Finish Scheme and Identification Markings, Ghost Scheme CF116D (CF-5 DUAL) AC".

This variation of the Ghost Aggressor variegated colour scheme featured the same FS.595 colours Grey 36251, Grey 36307, and Blue 35237 in a wraparound pattern encompassing both upper and lower surfaces.

The national markings featured a 16-inch roundel under the windscreen, a 140mm Canada Wordmark just aft of the engine intake, and a 100mm Canadian Forces Signature above the wing on both sides. A 12-inch Canadian Flag was displayed on each side of the vertical stabilizer, with the full Aircraft Serial Number under the flag in 4-inch numbers. A 16-inch roundel was applied, facing forward, on both the upper surface of the port wing and on the lower surface of the starboard wing. The Last Three Numbers of

the Aircraft Serial Number were applied in 10-inch numbers, facing forward, on both the upper surface of the starboard wing and on the lower surface of the port wing. All markings were in CGSB Grey 501-323. A false cockpit was painted on the undersurface of the nose, and the Last Two Numbers of the Aircraft Serial Number were applied on the interior and exterior surfaces of the nosewheel door, both in CGSB Grey 501-302 (not in evidence in photos).

5.9.4: CF-5D Ghost Aggressor Variegated Colour Scheme with Definitive Federal Identity Program Markings

This finish scheme was documented on the Canadian Forces Drawing 8040262, "Finish Scheme and Identification Markings, Ghost Scheme CF116D (CF-5 DUAL) AC".

This variation of the Ghost Aggressor variegated colour scheme featured the same FS.595 colours Grey 36251, Grey 36307, and Blue 35237 in a wraparound pattern encompassing both upper and lower surfaces.

CF-5D 116814 in the Ghost Aggressor variegated colour scheme with difinitive Federal Identity Program markings at Bristol Aerospace Ltd., Winnipeg International Airport.

(Bristol Aerospace Ltd. 13223-4)

The national markings featured a 12-inch roundel just aft of the engine intake, a 140mm Canada Wordmark above the wing, and a 100mm Canadian Forces Signature on the nose forward of the windscreen on both sides. A 20-inch Canadian Flag was displayed on each side of the vertical stabilizer, with the full Aircraft Serial Number under the flag in 4-inch numbers. A 16-inch roundel was applied, facing forward, on both the upper surface of the port wing and on the lower surface of the starboard wing. The Last Three Numbers of the Aircraft Serial Number were applied in 10-inch numbers, facing forward, on both the upper surface of the starboard wing, and on the lower surface of the port wing. All markings were in CGSB Grey 501-323. A false cockpit was painted on the undersurface of the nose, and the Last Two Numbers of the Aircraft Serial Number were applied on the interior and exterior surfaces of the nosewheel door, both in CGSB Grey 501-302.

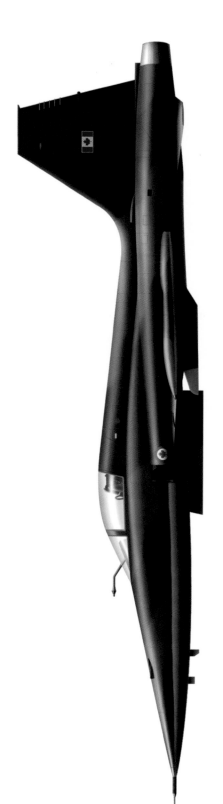

CF-5A 116768 in the three-colour variegated camouflage colour scheme with bilingual markings.

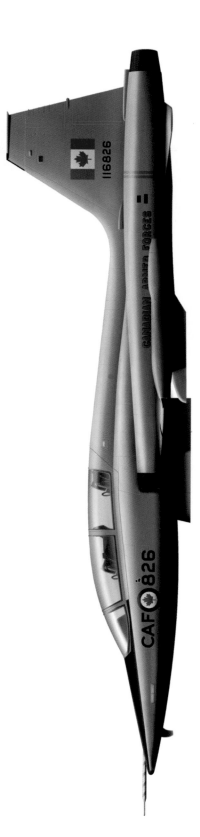

CF-5D 116826 in the aluminum colour scheme with bilingual markings.

Illustrations by Stephen Otvos

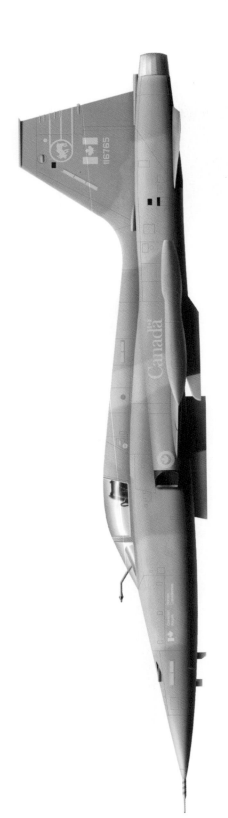

CF-5A 116765 in the Ghost Aggressor variegated colour scheme with Federal Identity Program markings.

CF-5D 116807 in the in the Grape Aggressor variegated colour scheme with original markings.

Illustrations by Stephen Otvos

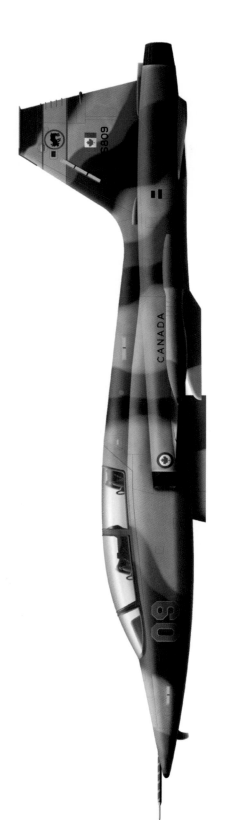

CF5D 116809 in the Lizard Aggressor wraparound variegated colour scheme with original markings.

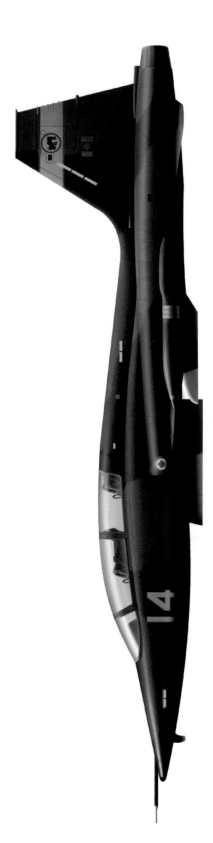

CF-5D 116814 in two-colour wraparound variegated colour scheme with full colour markings.

Illustrations by Stephen Otvos

Aircraft Armament Configurations

Underside view of CF-5A 116715 showing centreline weapons carrier and Mk.82 "Snakeye" bombs mounted on underwing pylons.

(DND, Neg. No.AEC 89-735)

Both the CF-5A and CF-5D were capable of carrying a wide variety of armament combinations, as illustrated by the table diagram and drawings and photographs of individual armament and equipment types. Only the CF-5A had the internally mounted M-39 cannon.

Armament combinations carried on weapon stations of CF-5A and CF-5D aircraft.

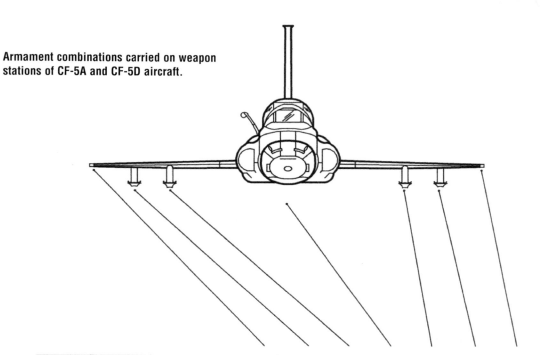

STORES	TIPS	OUTBD	INBD	CL	INBD	OUTBD	TIP
AIM-9/CATM-9/AIS Pod P4 ×	1						1
M-117 750-LB GP Bomb		1	1	1	1	1	
MK-82 500-LB Bomb (Low Drag)		1	1	1	1	1	
MK-82 500-LB Bomb (Snakeye)		1	1	1	1	1	
MK-83 1000-LB Bomb (Low Drag)			1	1	1		
MK-84 2000-LB Bomb (Low Drag)				1			
BL 755		1	1		1	1	
MK20 Rockeye		1	1		1	1	
LAU-5003		1	1		1	1	
LAU-5002		1	1		1	1	
SUU-20 Dispenser				1			
SUU-25 Dispenser		1	1		1	1	
TDU-10/B (Dart) Target						1	
RMU-10/A Tow Reel Pod				1			
125 Imp Gallon Fuel Tank			1	1	1		
42 Imp Gallon Fuel Tank	1						1
Luggage Carrier MXU-648/A ×				1			

- This figure indicates weapon station capabilities, not authorized weapon configurations.

× Not Shown

98

AIM-9/CATM-9 AIS Pod P4

LAU-5002

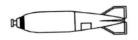

M117 Bomb

SUU-20 Dispenser

MK.82 Bomb (LD)

SUU-25 Dispenser

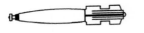

MK.82 Bomb (Snakeye)

RMU-10/A Tow ReelPod

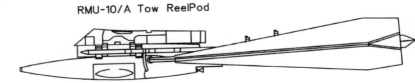

TDU-10/B (Dart) Target

MK.83 Bomb (LD)

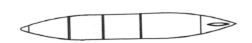

125 Imp Gallon Fuel Tank (CL)

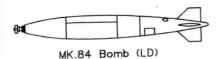

MK.84 Bomb (LD)

125 Imp Gallon Fuel Tank (INBD)

BL 755

42 Imp Gallon Fuel Tank

MK.20 Rockeye

Illustrations of armament types as listed on page 98.

LAU-5003

Port side weapon compartment in nose of CF-5A showing one of the two internally mounted M-39 cannon.

(A. Stachiw)

Starboard side weapon compartment in nose of CF-5A showing M-39 cannon with ammunition linkage.

(A. Stachiw)

Mk.82 500 lb. GP Bomb (Low Drag).

(A. Stachiw)

Mk.82 500 lb. Bomb (Snakeye).

(A. Stachiw)

BLU 755 (1/B)
Fire Bomb.

(A. Stachiw)

SUU-20 Bomb &
Rocket Dispenser
with 6 Practice
Bombs and four
2.75-inch Rockets.

(A. Stachiw)

LAU-5003 Rocket Pod with SUU-20 Bomb & Rocket Dispenser.

(A. Stachiw)

125 Imperial Gallon centreline fuel tank.

(A. Stachiw)

42 Imperial Gallon Tip Tank and 125 Imperial Gallon Underwing Pylon Tank. *(A. Stachiw)*

CF-5D 116817 in service with 419 F(T) Squadron with RMU-10/A Tow Reel Pod and TDU-10/B DART Target mounted under the port wing. *(A. Stachiw)*

TLD 1179 Armament Up and Down Load Kit for CF-5A/D aircraft.

(A. Stachiw)

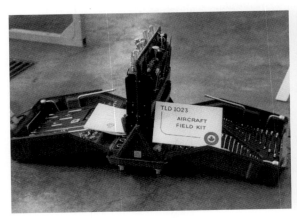

TLD 1023 CF-5A/D Aircraft Field Kit.

(A. Stachiw)

TLD 1176 CF-5A/D Aircraft Supplementary Kit.

(A. Stachiw)

CHAPTER SEVEN

Modelling the CF-5 Freedom Fighter

Model of CF-5D 116819 of 419 F(T) Sqn in the Lizard variegated finish scheme. Revell (Germany) issue of the Matchbox F-5B kit built by Vic Scheuerman features the Mike Grant Decals CF-5 sheet. A basic scratchbuilt cockpit was added, with crew members from the spares box, and the air intakes were added to the aft fuselage.

(Vic Schuerman)

Models in 1:72 Scale

Since the aircraft was first introduced in the late 1950s, kits of the F-5 have been produced by several manufacturers over the years. The finest representation, in 1:72 scale, was the series of F-5 kits introduced by Esci, which provided both a standard configured F-5A and the reconnaissance nose RF-5A, as well as a CF116D/F-5B. These kits all featured the tip tanks, which were almost always carried on the Canadian aircraft. The F-5A by Italaeri, released in 2002,

is probably a reissue of the Esci F-5A, and would be the recommended kit to use to represent the CF-5A if the modeller is not able to find Esci kits. The Matchbox F-5A and F-5B were accurate in shape and dimension, although handicapped by the heavy panel lines and lack of detail, but could serve the purpose with a certain amount of effort. They featured the peanut shaped tip tanks characteristic of the F-5A/B series. The Hasegawa kits (also released by Frog) of the F-5A and T-38 Talon would also be suitable, but lack the tip tanks. The F-5A by Airfix, is accurate but very basic, and does not feature the tip tanks.

Model of CF-5A 116703, in the markings of 419 F(T) Squadron Presentation Aircraft "Bruce the Moose". The Esci F-5A kit built by Bill Scobie with Arrow Graphics decal.

(Bill Scobie)

Model of CF-5D 116837, in the markings of 434 TAC(F) Sqn, in standard aluminum finish scheme. The Hasegawa T-38 kit built by Bill Scobie with Flight Colours decal.

(Bill Scobie)

MODEL KITS:

Airfix F-5A: available, a basic representation of the aircraft, no tip tanks

Esci F-5A: was excellent representation of aircraft, featured tip tanks

Esci F-5C / RF-5A: no longer available; was excellent representation of aircraft, featured tip tanks

Esci CF-116 / F-5B: was excellent representation of aircraft, featured tip tanks

Hasegawa F-5A: up to early Hasegawa standards, no tip tanks

Hasegawa T-38: up to early Hasegawa standards

Italaeri F-5A: former Esci F-5A

Matchbox F-5A: a good basic representation of the aircraft, featured tip tanks

Matchbox F-5B/CF116D: a good basic representation of the aircraft, featured tip tanks

DECALS:

Arrow Graphics: Decal 72-featured 419 Presentation Aircraft 116703 "Bruce the Moose"

Flight Colours: No longer available, depicted 6 aircraft, both CF-5A and CF-5D.

JBOT Decals (*http://members.rogers.com/jbot6/*)

Has prepared a series of decal sheets depicting CF-5 aircraft. These represent:
1. CF-5A in both the two colour wraparound scheme with subdued markings, and the "Ghost" low viz scheme.
2. CF-5A 116703, 419 Fighter Training Squadron "Bruce the Moose" , 1st presentation aircraft;
3. CF-5A 116721, 419 Fighter Training Squadron "Bruce the Moose" ,2nd presentation aircraft;
4. CF-5A 116743, 419 Fighter Training Squadron "Bruce the Moose" ,3rd presentation aircraft.

Leading Edge Decals (*http://lemdecal.com/*)

CF-5 sheets are in preparation at the time of writing

Mike Grant Decals (*http://www.cadvision.com/mikegrant/MikeGrantDecals/*)

Offers a CF-5 decal sheet depicting Canadian CF-5s. The sheet provides markings for four aircraft, including some stencilling:
1. CF-5A 116753, 434 "Bluenose" TAC(F) Sqn in the 2 colour wraparound scheme with toned down markings, CFB Bagotville;
2. CF-5D 116837, 1 CFFTS, CFB Cold Lake, in original aluminum finish scheme;
3. CF-5A 116705, 419 "Moose" Fighter Training Squadron, CFB Cold Lake in "Ghost" Aggressor scheme;
4. CF-5D 116819, 419 "Moose" Fighter Training Squadron, CFB Cold Lake in "Ghost" Aggressor scheme.

Sabre Decals: No longer available, depicted 2 aircraft, both CF-5A and CF-5D, along with CF104 Starfighter

AFTER MARKET PRODUCTS:

Hasegawa: Hasegawa Weapon Set Kits offer many weapons applicable to CF-5A/D.

Models in 1:48 Scale

In 1:48 scale, the Testors / Hawk F-5A (also released by Italaeri) is the only available kit that represents the CF- 5A. While it is accurate in shape and dimension, it is very basic, lacking in detail, and is without tip tanks. This shortcoming can be remedied by purchasing the Missing Link Models resin tip tanks. For the more adventurous modeller, grafting the nose section of the Monogram F-5E Tiger II from the canted bulkhead forward onto the basic Testors F-5A fuselage will provide good cockpit detail (with minor inconsistencies to the CF-5A). There is a possibility of a resin conversion from Belcher Bits, using the F-5E from Monogram as the basic kit.

The Academy T-38, which was slated for 2002 release, can be converted to a CF-5D. The cockpit details from the Monogram F-5F could be used to make the cockpit more representative of a CF-5D.

MODEL KITS:

Academy T-38: slated for 2002 release.
Fujimi F-5A: a good basic representation of the aircraft (may be 1:50 scale)
Fujimi F-5B/T-38; a good basic representation of the aircraft (may be 1:50 scale)
Italaeri F-5A: a reissue of the Testors (Hawk) kit.
Monogram F-5E: an excellent representation of the aircraft (for conversion parts only).
Monogram F-5F: an excellent representation of the aircraft (for conversion parts only).
Testors/Hawk F-5A: a good basic representation of the aircraft; no tip tanks.

DECALS:

JBOT Decals *(http://members.rogers.com/jbot6/)*
See description of 1:72 Scale decals.

Leading Edge Decals: *(http://lemdecal.com/)*
See description of 1:72 Scale decals

Mike Grant Decals *(http://www.cadvision.com/mikegrant/MikeGrantDecals/)*
See description of 1:72 Scale decals

Sabre Decals: See description of 1:72 Scale decals

AFTER MARKET PRODUCTS:

Hasegawa: Hasegawa Weapon Set Kits offer many weapons applicable to CF-5A/D.

Missing Link Models: Offers F-5A tip tanks in resin.

Models in 1:32 Scale

In the absence of an F-5A model in 1:32 scale, the modeller is faced with the conversion of the 1:32 scale Hasegawa F-5E kit (also released by Revell Germany). This conversion was done by John Lumley of Winnipeg, Manitoba and fully described in his article, which appeared in *Scale Modeler* magazine in the November 1993 issue. John has since prepared a master for a resin conversion kit, with assistance by Scott Anningson.

This conversion will be produced and marketed by Mike Belcher in his Belcher Bits resin conversion series for 2003 release.

Hasegawa F-5E: Excellent representation of F-5E aircraft to the usual Hasegawa standard. This kit requires extensive modification to represent the Canadair CF-5A as previously noted.

DECALS:

JBOT Decals (*http://members.rogers.com/jbot6/*)
See description of 1:72 Scale decals

After Market Products:
Custom Aeronautical Miniatures: CAMR 32019 Mk.82 Bomb
CAMR 32020 Mk.82 Snakeye Bomb
CAMR 32023 M-117 750 lb. GP Bomb
CAMR 32024/32053 Rockeye Cluster Bombs
CAMR 32032 F-5E Resin ejection seat

Verlinden: Offers a photoetch detail and resin cockpit set #1739 which is in general applicable to the CF-5A.

Black Box; Resin upgrade set 32010 for F-5E kit, which is in general applicable to the CF-5A.

Model of CF-5A 116751, 434 "Bluenose" TAC(F) Squadron aircraft. Conversion of Hasegawa F-5E kit by John Lumley with custom decals. *(John Lumley)*

BIBLIOGRAPHY

"408 Squadron History." Belleville: Hangar Bookshelf, 1984.

"433 Squadron History." Belleville: Hangar Bookshelf, 1985.

"434 Squadron History." Belleville: Hangar Bookshelf, 1984.

Archer, Robert D. "Northrop N-156F Freedom Fighter." *Flight* (January 8, 1960): 43-50

Canadair CF-5 Canadian Profile. Ottawa: Sabre Model Supplies Publishing,1985.

Evans, Stanley H. "Northrop N-156F Freedom Fighter." *The Aeroplane and Astronautics Magazine* (December 4, 1959): 573-578.

Kostenuk, S., and J. Griffin. *RCAF Squadron Histories and Aircraft*. Ottawa: National Museum of Man, 1980.

Martin, Patrick. *Canadian Armed Forces, Aircraft Finish & Markings, 1968-1997*. Self published, 1997

"'Moosemen,' 419 Squadron History." CFB Cold Lake, AB: 419 Squadron, 1989.

Stachiw, Anthony. "In Canadian Service CF-5 Freedom Fighter." *Airforce* (1986).